What people are saying about *Learning to Follow Jesus*:

"I've always felt like there was a lack of resources to help new believers take their first steps following Christ. Daniel McNaughton fills the gap with *Learning to Follow Jesus*. It will point new believers in the right direction." —**Mark Batterson,** author of *In a Pit with a Lion on a Snowy Day*, *Wild Goose Chase*, and *Primal* (www.evotional.com).

"The search for a biblically faithful and culturally relevant discipleship tool is over. *Learning to Follow Jesus* is the right book in the right place at the right time. Easy to understand and use, *LFJ* is an ideal resource for supporting the spiritual growth of those new, and not-so-new, to faith." — **Earl Creps**, author of *Off-Road Disciplines* and *Reverse Mentoring*.

"Learn. Relearn. Never stop learning, to follow Jesus. Step by step, this book is a journey that simplifies and makes accessible the best relationship of your life. Be the student, be the coach, and do it all over again. Allow yourself to be discipled, you'll never be the same." — **Juliet Richardson**, recording artist.

"Of all the books that I have read in the last two years, this book is the book I believe will make the greatest impact for the Kingdom of God. We should be about making disciples and this book gives us a pathway to make this happen in our churches." — **Joel Hunter,** Pastor of Northwood Assembly and Director of Discovery for Church Multiplication Network.

D1621789

Learning to Follow Jesus

One Step at a Time

Learning to Follow Jesus
One Step at a Time

by
Daniel McNaughton
and
Trinity Jordan

www.elevation.cc

Morning Joy Media
Spring City, Pennsylvania

Published by Morning Joy Media.

Visit www.morningjoymedia.com for more information on bulk discounts and special promotions, or e-mail your questions to info@morningjoymedia.com.

Unless otherwise noted, Scripture quotations are taken from the Holy Bible, New International Version®, NIV®. Copyright © 1973, 1978, 1984 by Biblica, Inc.™ Used by permission of Zondervan. All rights reserved worldwide.

Scripture quotations marked KJV are from the King James Version.

Scripture quotations marked NCV taken from the New Century Version. Copyright © 2005 by Thomas Nelson, Inc. Used by permission. All rights reserved.

The coaching model adopted in this resource, particularly the 5Rs of coaching, comes from *Coaching 101* by Robert E. Logan, Sherilyn Carlton, and Tara Miller. (ChurchSmart Resources, 2003). Used by permission.

The Evangelism Styles Questionnaire was taken from **Becoming a Contagious Christian Participant's Guide** by LEE P. STROBEL; BILL HYBELS; MARK MITTELBERG. Copyright © 1995, 2007 by Willow Creek Community Church. Used by permission of Zondervan. WWW.ZONDERVAN.COM.

The assessments in Step 1 through Step 4 and "God's Answer for Four Common Lies" in Resources Attribute Five were reprinted from *The Search for Significance* by Robert S. McGee (Rapha Publishing, 1985). Used by permission.

Cover Design: Brandon Irwin (brandon@elevation.cc)
Interior Design: Debbie Capeci
Author Photos: Dan Desrosiers and Brandon Irwin

Subject Headings:
1. Discipling (Christianity) 2. Spiritual formation. 3. Christian life.

ISBN 978-0-9826102-2-0

Printed in the United States of America

This book is dedicated to

my Dad, who gave me my first Bible and gave me
a foundation of believing in Jesus,

and to my spiritual mentors:

Steve Pike, Doyle Robinson, and Jim Ladd.
I see Jesus in the way you live and you have helped me live
just like Him.

—Trinity Jordan

*Note: Unless otherwise indicated, the first-person pronouns
occurring in individual stories and situational examples refer to
Trinity Jordan, and those occurring in instructional passages refer
to Daniel McNaughton.*

Contents

Acknowledgements

I (TRINITY) MET DANIEL MCNAUGHTON AT VALLEY FORGE when I came to speak at a college event. It wasn't too long after that I found myself at two other colleges speaking with Daniel. We had a lot in common: both very good looking, both very smart, both athletic, and both very humble. We hit it off and formed a friendship that brought us to working together.

This book is the brainchild of Daniel McNaughton. His leadership and writings have created this book you are holding right now. I am honored to work with a godly man like Daniel and honored to be invited to be part of this project.

Everything I have to write or teach isn't my own. It is what I have read from God's Word and what I have learned from God's people. I borrowed from some amazing godly people, because they have helped me in my journey with Jesus.

First, I want to give all glory and honor to Messiah Jesus. Everything I do in life is for him.

There is no one closer to me on this planet than my best friend: my wife, Ami. I thank God that he blinded her eyes for about a year until I was able to enter into a covenant with her. She is a gift from God. Her support and love is golden. She keeps me humble and not believing my own press. I love her!

My daughters became my inspiration as I continually thought about what they needed to learn as they followed Jesus in life. I am thankful that God has granted them to me and Ami in this life and let us be their parents and stewards.

Ministry has always been about helping others learn to follow Jesus. I am honored to work with some of the best people out there. Every leader and staff member at Elevation Church has poured themselves into my life. I keep telling them that I want to do ministry with them for the rest of our lives and grow old with them; I am sure they will eventually get tired of me. The leaders of Elevation have taught me so much that has been written about in these pages. Brandon Irwin keeps me creative and authentic. Brendan Perko has taught me more about relationships than anyone I know. Ryan Lind has taught me grace. Brian Yocum is the most loyal person I know and has taught me how to be a true friend. Jenny Daniels has shown me how far God can reach to save us. Byron Marshall keeps humility and love in my face. Ryan Eaves taught me forgiveness. I am grateful to these men and women.

This book grew out of authentic community at two churches: one in Pennsylvania, Spring Valley Community Church, and one in Utah, Elevation Church. I am honored to be part of Elevation.

I want to acknowledge that my portions of this writing were done at Starbucks in Layton, Utah, and the Allegro Papagyo Resort in Costo Rica; and all my writing was done on a Mac. (Steve Jobs and Howard Schultz, I would love some free stuff now.)

Finally, I want to say that God is the one who put this together with a lot of people that I have never met and people I have; this truly is the body of Christ in action here on earth. I pray that this book will be a continuation of the words Jesus gave to his disciples before he ascended to heaven, "Go and make disciples..."

Introduction

I (DANIEL) WILL NEVER FORGET sitting in my office at a church in Toronto, Ontario, where I served as an assistant pastor when it dawned on me that I had never been systematically and intentionally shown how to become a disciple, a fully-devoted follower of Jesus. It was shocking to realize the irony. I was raised in a Christian home, attended many Christian meetings, graduated from a denominational college with a degree in Bible, received a masters degree from a reputable seminary, completed more than half of my Ph.D. in Biblical Studies, and was serving as a pastor, but I was never shown how to systematically disciple people. I had invited Christ into my life and was attempting to follow Jesus to the best of my ability, but it was fuzzy. What is a disciple? What does a disciple look like? What does a disciple do?

This was especially disturbing to me because the Gospel of Matthew concludes with the resurrected Jesus appearing to his followers giving them only one command in the Great Commission. It is not "go" as I had often heard preached. It is "make disciples." One command! Why was it fuzzy?

Over the past eighteen years, I have asked many of my friends if they can clearly and succinctly describe what a disciple is and how to make one. Unfortunately, most are like I was...fuzzy. That does not mean we are not making disciples. It is just not clear. Rather than rant about how this could be, I decided to go on a quest to learn how. We cannot change the past, but we can be part of a future that rediscovers what Jesus had in mind when he gave the one command.

This book is designed to be a simple, practical guide

for those who want to learn to follow Jesus. There are four main parts to the guide: an overview of the seven essential attributes of the follower of Jesus (also called "First Steps"); a step-by-step development of each attribute; resources to augment each attribute; and spiritual coaching guides. To get the most out of this book, you will need to read the biblical passages, memorize the Scriptures, write out your answers in the book, pray the prayers, and discuss your progress with a spiritual coach. The goal is not simply to complete the book. The goal is that you will be growing in each of the seven attributes for the rest of your life. When you finish working through the guide one time and are growing in each attribute, you are ready to come alongside another person to help him or her learn to follow Jesus. Keep it going! If you help one person a year follow Jesus and if each person you help does the same, and those they help do the same, in thirty-three years we could reach the entire world with the gospel. I want be part of a worldwide movement of people who focus their lives on the "one thing" that matters most to Jesus. How about you?

Getting Started

CONGRATULATIONS ON YOUR DECISION to become a follower of Jesus! You may or may not realize it yet, but following Jesus is the most important decision you will ever make in your life. It will affect every future decision you will make on this earth, and it will affect where you spend eternity. You have made a great decision! This book is designed to help you develop in your walk with Christ so you can know and honor God the rest of your life and for eternity.

Since it is such an important decision, it is worthwhile to take a few minutes to review what it means to become a follower of Jesus. John 1:12 describes becoming part of God's family as a two-part decision: "Yet to all who received him [Jesus], to those who believed in his name, he gave the right to become children of God." You must **receive** Christ and **believe** in his name. Even though the Bible teaches that Jesus created the universe (John 1:3), he never forces anyone to follow him. God gives you freedom to accept or reject Jesus. By receiving Jesus, you accept that he was God, that he was the perfect representation of what God is like. By believing in his name, you are trusting that Jesus paid the price for your sin when he died on the cross. John 3:16 says, "For God so loved the world that he gave his one and only Son, that whoever believes in him shall not perish but have eternal life." God came to earth because he loves every one of us and wants us to have eternal life. Jesus describes eternal life this way in John 17:3, "Now this is eternal life: that they may know you, the only true God, and Jesus Christ, whom you have sent." Eternal life is knowing Jesus. If you are uncertain whether or not you have done that, why not take a minute right now and make sure. If you are unaccustomed to praying or if you are unsure what to pray, you can join me in the following prayer.

> ### Prayer:
> Dear Heavenly Father, I want to become a follower of Jesus. I receive Jesus into my life. I believe he was God and that he came to pay the price for my sin when he died on the cross. Please forgive me for living life my own way. I turn away from that life and I turn toward you. As best I know how and with your help, I want to live for you from this day forward. Amen.

Having received Jesus and believed what he came to do, you can now be certain that you are part of God's family.

There are a few things that are important to keep in mind from the beginning. First, becoming a follower of Jesus is not just about learning information. It is much more than that. Jesus said that those who come to him, hear his words, and put them into practice will be the ones who will have a foundation on which to stand when tough times come. Building a solid foundation requires you to bring everything to Christ, hear God's Word, and then put it into practice.

Second, most of us learn best from watching and learning from others. In other words, "more is caught than is taught." That's why we encourage you to put yourself in four contexts where you can learn from others: a large gathering where you can worship God and hear Bible teaching (a church service); a house church or small group where you can apply the Bible to your life and live out your faith with others; a one-on-one mentoring meeting with a spiritual coach; and a private time with God on your own. *Learning to Follow Jesus* is a tool that can help you develop in your private time with God and can serve as a discussion starter with you and your coach. We all need people with whom we can share our honest thoughts, our successes, our failures, and our questions, especially when we are just starting out on a new venture. A spiritual coach and the people in your small group or house church will help you learn how to honor God in every area of life. They will probably not have all the answers to your questions, but they may serve as resources to you, and they are committed to sharing what they know with you.

What church do you plan to attend?.............................

Would you like a spiritual coach?...............................

Would you like more information about small groups?....

If you don't have a spiritual coach or a small group yet, please contact a pastor to help you find both.

Third, following Christ is a process. You will not be perfect, nor will your spiritual coach or the members of your small group. Only Jesus is perfect. When you follow Christ, you accept what he has done for you. Knowing that your eternal destiny depends on Jesus' righteousness and not yours will set you free from trying to work to get God to love you. Jesus has already pleased God for you. There is nothing you can ever do to make God love you more. His love for you is limitless and eternal. His thoughts about you are always good. Enjoy your newfound reality of knowing God is pleased with you because of Jesus. Don't try to work to please him. Just live your life in gratitude for his amazing love and acceptance. As you spend time with other followers of Christ and with your loving Heavenly Father, you will discover that you want to become more like Christ, and you will change. God will change you.

This book is designed to help you cultivate good habits that will support a healthy spiritual environment for your new walk with Christ. To get the most out of this tool, you will need to make the following choices:

→ Set aside about fifteen minutes per day to focus on your spiritual growth. Every relationship takes time. Your relationship with Christ is no exception. Choose a time slot that will work consistently for you. Many people find that the morning is best. Others believe the time before they go to bed is best. Some people do both. The most important thing is that you make time for your spiritual growth. You may have to experiment but pick a time that works for you. What time will work best for you on a daily basis?

....

→ Write your answers in the book. You will retain more of what you are learning if you take the time to write your answers.

→ Read the Bible references for yourself. If you don't have a Bible in a modern translation (New International Version [NIV] and New Living Translation [NLT] are good ones), ask your spiritual coach to help you find one. What translation will you use?

....

→ Memorize the verses linked with each attribute. Do your best to learn them word-for-word. If you take a little time each day, you will discover they will come to mind much easier. Review all previously memorized verses daily; that puts them into your long-term memory. You won't regret it.

→ Put what you learn into practice right away. A follower of Jesus is one who learns what Jesus is like and then takes action to become like him. Enjoy the journey.

First Steps

•

An Overview
of the Attributes

Attribute One • Overview
Learn to Be With Jesus

Scripture Memory (new):

"Come, follow me," Jesus said, "and I will make you fishers of men." Matthew 4:19

Read: Matthew 4:18–22

O NE OF THE FIRST THINGS we learn when we become followers of Jesus is he wants us to be with him.

What did Jesus say to Peter and Andrew in Matthew 4:18–22? ....

....

Notice that Jesus took the initiative in their relationship. He loved them and he loves you as well. He is and has been reaching out to you from the time you were born. He invites you to follow him—to be with him.

In John's Gospel in chapter 1, we also see Jesus inviting people to be with him. Andrew started following Jesus after John the Baptist said Jesus was "the Lamb of God who takes away the sin of the world." When Jesus saw Andrew following him, he asked, "What do you want?" Andrew responded by calling Jesus "Teacher" and asking where he was staying. Jesus invited him, "Come and see" and they spent the whole day together. There is no higher calling in life than Jesus' call to be with him. You may do great things for him. You may help many people learn to follow him and that's great, but your primary calling is just to be with Jesus.

Does it surprise you that the Creator of the universe invites us to be with him? The psalmist writes, "What is man that you are mindful of him, the son of man that you care for him?" (Psalm 8:4). God cares about you and wants you to be close to him. How does it make you feel to know that Jesus wants you to be with him? (Pause right now and take a few minutes to thank the Lord for calling you to follow him. Tell him how you feel and affirm your commitment to follow him.)

What are some of your feelings about Jesus' calling you to be one of his followers?..
....
....

What did Peter, Andrew, James and John have to leave behind to follow Jesus?...
....
....

What would be tough for you to leave behind to follow him?..
....

While it may seem tough to leave something behind right now, you will soon realize that nothing you leave behind can compare in value to the amazing gift that you have as a follower of Jesus.

In Matthew 13:44–46 Jesus compares finding the kingdom of God (having Christ rule in your heart) to a man who found a treasure in a field. He hid the treasure and then in his great joy went and sold all he had and bought that field. He also compared it to a merchant who found a pearl of great value and went away and sold everything he had and bought it. Nothing you have can compare with the treasure you have when you follow Jesus.

One of the best parts about following Jesus is that he will never leave you. The last words in the book of Matthew say this, "And surely I am with you always, to the very end of the age." Jesus' commitment to be with you is a forever thing. Though others leave you or don't fulfill their commitments to you, Jesus promises that he will always be with you both now and throughout eternity. You will never be alone again.

What did Jesus say would happen if Peter and Andrew followed him?...

....

....

Following Jesus will change your life. He promised to transform his disciples from being fishermen who could catch fish to fishermen who would catch people. He will transform your life as well so you can become the person he designed you to be. You may not know what that is just yet, but it will become clear as you follow him. There is one thing you can be sure of, however: Jesus will lead you to make a difference in the lives of others. That was his purpose for coming, and it was the one thing he told his disciples to do as he was leaving. Don't let that intimidate you. It will be a wonderful and fulfilling journey. He will show you the next steps, and he will always be with you. Just enjoy being with him now.

Prayer:
Heavenly Father, thank you for inviting me to follow you. It amazes me that you care about me enough to want to be with me. I respond to your invitation again and declare that I am your follower. I will joyfully leave behind the things you ask me to because I believe that I will be better off with you. Change me into the person you want me to become. I rest in your commitment to be with me forever. I also rest in your presence right now, my heart's true home. Amen.

Attribute Two • Overview
Learn to Listen

Scripture Memory:

"Come, _____ me," Jesus _____, "and I will make
you _____ of men." Matthew ____:19

*"Come, follow me," Jesus said, "and I will make you fishers of
men." Matthew 4:19*

Read: Matthew 4:23–25

J ESUS BEGAN TEACHING his followers by inviting them to
observe what he was doing. According to these verses, what
did the first followers of Jesus observe him doing?.................
....

As a follower of Jesus, it is important for you to observe
Jesus' teaching, preaching, and healing as well. (We'll talk
about Jesus' healing in the next attribute.) You will find a
summary of Jesus' preaching in Matthew 4:17: "From that
time on Jesus began to preach, 'Repent, for the kingdom
of heaven is near.'" There are a couple of terms that need
defining. First, the word "repent" means "to turn away
from something and to turn toward something else." When
some people hear the word "repent" they think of it nega-
tively. Perhaps it stirs up an image of a screaming evangelist.
Repentance, however, is positive. When we repent we get to
turn away from the things that are keeping us from following

Christ, and then turn to him, the Author of life.

Second, "the kingdom of heaven" means that God can have first place in your heart. I don't know what comes to your mind when you think of "kingdom," but I think of walled cities, castles and kings, like the Battle of Helms Deep in the movie *Lord of the Rings: The Two Towers*. The kingdom of heaven is different from that. God's kingdom is not about weapons and war machines, but there is a king. Luke 17:20b–21 states, "The kingdom of God does not come with your careful observation, nor will people say, 'Here it is,' or 'There it is,' because the kingdom of God is within you." When the kingdom of God comes in your life, he rules your heart. Your life will change, not by force but by the power of God. We can change because Jesus is near to help us and empower us. That's great news.

Matthew 4:23 describes Jesus' preaching about the kingdom like that. The fact that we can turn away from our old lives and have God rule in our hearts is great news. But it's not without a cost. Your priorities will change as you make room for God to rule in your life. You know what rules your heart by where you give your treasures: your time, your talent, and your money.

What would you say are the top priorities in your life right now? ....
....

What are some things you need to turn away from (repent) so that Christ can rule in your heart? ....
....

Repentance is ongoing for a follower of Christ. No one will ever be perfect except Jesus. As you get to know Jesus better, repentance will become easier because you will realize that his ways are always best!

What good things could happen if you were to repent from these things? ....

What are some things from which you would like to repent?

I want to repent from: I can turn from this and to God by:

1............................   ....

2............................   ....

3............................   ....

You may want to share these with your spiritual coach, who can encourage you in your decisions. Your spiritual coach is going through the same process, so you don't need to worry about what he or she will think of you. Romans 3:23 reminds us that "All have sinned and fall short of the glory of God." There's another great passage about this as well in 1 John 1:8–10:

> If we claim to be without sin, we deceive ourselves and the truth is not in us. If we confess our sins, he is faithful and just and will forgive us our sins and purify us from all unrighteousness. If we claim we have not sinned, we make him out to be a liar and his word has no place in our lives.

Repentance just brings these things to light so we can deal with them, with God's help. Remember, he is with you.

Prayer:

Dear Jesus, thank you for the invitation to turn away from my old life. I do actively turn away from the things I have done that are wrong and I turn to you. I repent from [tell God the things you mentioned previously]. Thank you for replacing those things with your leadership in my life. I welcome you into my life. Thank you also for inviting me to bring my pain to you. Please bring healing to my life in every way. I am so grateful to you for helping me find life in you, Jesus Christ. Amen.

Attribute Three • Overview
Learn to Heal

Scripture Memory:
" _____ , follow _____ ," Jesus said, " _____ I will _____
you fishers of _____ ." Matthew ___ : ___

"Come, follow me," Jesus said, "and I will make you fishers of men." Matthew 4:19

Read: Matthew 4:23–25

As I was looking at Jesus' method for helping people learn to follow him, it struck me that one of the first things he did was invite his followers to be with him while he preached and healed people. There is nothing like seeing God heal firsthand. Based on these verses, what kinds of things did Jesus heal?[1] ....

....

When I first began traveling and speaking at different churches across the United States, I was invited to speak at a church in Virginia to do a "healing service." I had never been to a healing service let alone speak at one, which meant I didn't have a clue what was expected of me.

When I got to the church service I spoke as I always did about Jesus and how we can trust him over all the things of this world. At the end of the service I invited people to come forward if they needed Jesus to heal them.

A lot of people came forward, but as I was praying with one lady I thought of my own allergy. If Jesus could heal them, why not me? Right there I asked Jesus to heal me and I never had any more troubles with my allergy.

I was skeptical of all the healings I had heard about when I was a new follower of Jesus. One of my professors at Texas Christian University used to say to us that Jesus' miracles were just legends that had developed. I remember asking a pastor at a local church if he believed Jesus could heal today and he told me that Jesus doesn't do that anymore.

All of the philosophical talk of why Jesus didn't heal went out the window for me when I experienced it on my own. Be open to God's supernatural intervention in your life. Don't try to fake anything. It is not like magic. You don't have to say the right words in your prayer, and you don't have to work yourself up emotionally to receive a miracle. Just ask God to do the miraculous and see what happens.

While you are pondering that thought, consider that there are eighty-eight references in the New Testament to healing. Some of them are stories of Jesus healing someone. Others, however, refer to God healing people through the prayers of his followers (Luke 9:2, 9:6; Acts 3:16, 4:9–30, 5:16, 8:7, 9:34, 10:38, 14:9, 28:8). In fact, 1 Corinthians 12:9 refers to "gifts of healing" being given to some of Christ's followers. You need to know that since Christ lives in you, he can provide healing through you. Begin to pray and ask him to meet needs about which you are aware.

We all need healing. You may need physical or emotional healing. You might need healing in a relationship. We all need spiritual healing. Whatever your need, you can bring it to the Lord and ask him. I wish I understood why God chooses to heal sometimes and not others, but I do not. But you never want it to be said about you that you could have had healing but you didn't ask. So ask and trust God.

What kinds of things do you need healing for today?

....

....

....

Share these with your spiritual coach, who will agree with you in prayer for your healing.

Prayer:
Thank you, Heavenly Father, for reminding me that you care about the details of my life. I praise you and thank you for the new life you are giving me through Jesus. In response to what I am reading today, I ask you for healing for [name the areas for which you want healing]. (Describe how the problem has caused you pain or suffering. Tell it to God even though he already knows.) Your Word tells me that you are compassionate toward me and that you care about me. I ask that you would have mercy on me about [name the area]. I trust that you love me and care about me. Thank you for your kindness to me. In Jesus' name I pray, amen.

Attribute Four • Overview
Learn to Influence

Scripture Memory:

"Come, _____ _____," Jesus said, " _____ _____
_____ _____ you _____ of men." _____ _____:_____

"Come, follow me," Jesus said, "and I will make you fishers of men." Matthew 4:19

Read: Matthew 5:13–16

WHO ARE YOU? And why are you here? Many people spend their whole lives not ever knowing why they are on the planet. At the beginning of his teaching Jesus clearly defines who we are as his followers.

What two metaphors does Jesus use to describe his followers?..
....

Both of these metaphors describe our identity as influencers for God. Salt preserves things and makes our food taste better. When it comes in contact with something it has an effect. Light helps us see things more clearly, especially when it is dark. The reason we are on this planet is to impact people for God. We are not here for ourselves. As Rick Warren so aptly puts it:

> It's not about you. The purpose of your life is far greater than your own personal fulfillment, your peace of mind, or even your happiness. It's far greater than your family, your career, or

even your wildest dreams and ambitions. If you want to know why you were placed on this planet, you must start with God. You were born by his purpose and for his purpose.[1]

The ultimate goal for everything you do is to influence people for God so they might also praise God in heaven. You are an attractor for God.

This thought could be a bit overwhelming. You might say, "How can I ever attract people to God? My life is not perfect enough to point people to God." The answer? God will attract people to himself through your life as you continue to learn to follow him. Of course you are not perfect, but he is. As God begins to change you, people will notice and they may want to know how that happened.

Have you ever noticed that when you hang out with someone you become like them? Do you have a friend with whom you share special vocabulary or a favorite handshake or similar jokes? The same will become true with you and Jesus. As you are with him, you will start to become more and more like him. For most of us, this is such a gradual process that we may not even see it, but others will. And when they do, we are living up to our identity as salt and light.

Make a list of friends, family, neighbors, and co-workers who could benefit from becoming followers of Jesus.

....
....
....
....
....
....
....
....
....
....

Prayer:

Heavenly Father, thank you for defining who I am and why I'm on this planet. Life is starting to make sense. I really want you to influence people through my life. Continue to change me so that I reflect you clearly. I know I can't do this on my own and you are not asking me to. I rest in our relationship right now. You are so good. I bring my friends and family to you now. Would you pull them to you? Would you open their eyes to see how empty their lives are without you? Would you help them see their need for a forever relationship with you? Remove any confusion or barriers that would keep them from getting to know you. Help my life to be attractive for you. Give me wisdom to know how to approach these relationships. Help me to love them. I bring them to you. Amen.

Attribute Five • Overview
Learn to Love

Scripture Memory:

"Come, _____ ___ ," _____ ___ , "and I __

___ ___ ___ ___ ___ ." _____ ___ : ___

"Come, follow me," Jesus said, "and I will make you fishers of men." Matthew 4:19

Read: Matthew 5:43–48

FOLLOWERS OF JESUS LEARN from the beginning and all throughout their lives that love is the foundation for everything. Many people think that loving God is only a personal and private thing. While loving God is both personal and private, it is not only that. Loving God will also lead you to love people. What two commands does Jesus make in Matthew 5:44?...

....

If you wrote, "love your enemies" and "pray for those who persecute you," you are correct. According to Matthew 5:45, what does Jesus say will happen if we obey him in these commands?...

....

One thing that identifies an authentic follower of Jesus is love for others. As you are learning to follow, it may seem quite foreign to you that you could love people who have hurt you. If you have people who have caused you pain in your past whom you find difficult to love, I have good news for you. Jesus will enable you to rise above your past hurts. As you get to know Jesus better and as you learn to trust and obey him, you will find great freedom. *Learning to Follow Jesus* can help you take steps in that direction.[1] You will pour out your heart to God and you will enjoy the kindness and the compassion of God as he heals you.

Today's challenge, however, is actually a decision only you can make. Will you obey Jesus' commands in Matthew 5:43–48 to love your enemies and pray for those who persecute you? As you are thinking about this, I want you to know a couple of things. First, the type of love Jesus is talking about is not a feeling. Love means you do what is best for the other person regardless of how you or they feel about it. It is choosing to see that person as someone Jesus loves. As such, it is a decision. Choosing to love someone who had hurt me would never have happened in my life if Jesus did not teach me to do it. I would never have considered it. It is not logical or normal for me to do good to my enemies. Second, loving someone does not necessarily mean that you do what the other person wants. That would not always be loving. For example, it is not the most loving thing to allow abusive people to continue to abuse you. The most loving thing might be for you to help those people experience the consequences of their actions. Third, the only way you are going to be able to love people the way they need to be loved, especially your enemies, is with Jesus' help. That's why you pray for them. Tell God your honest feelings about those people and what you want to happen to them (good or bad).

As you open up this dialogue with God, a wonderful thing will happen. Your capacity to love God will grow as will your capacity to love people. You will also discover that your responses to people can be independent of their actions and their responses toward you. You may even find yourself starting to feel compassion toward them. You may not like them, but you will be able to love them. I have found great freedom in knowing I do not have to hate my enemies anymore.

Having encouraged you, it is time now to act. For whom do you need to pray?..

....

Join with me now as we pray.

Prayer:

Heavenly Father, you are challenging me today to do something that goes against my nature, to love my enemies. I confess I have not done that in the past, but I want to learn from you how to do that. I pray now for [mention the person's name]. [Say his name] became my enemy when he [tell God what the person did to hurt you even though God already knows.] You know how that hurt me and the decisions I made because of that. I bring that to you right now. Continue the healing process in my life. I know that you love [mention the name] and that you want the best for his life. I ask that your plan for him will be accomplished. Help me to act in loving ways toward [name] in the future. Teach me how to love like you love. Amen.

Attribute Six • Overview
Learn to Pray

Scripture Memory:

" ———————, ——— ——, " ——— ———, " ——— ———
——— ——— ——— ——— ——— ———.
——— ——— : ———

"Come, follow me," Jesus said, "and I will make you fishers of men." Matthew 4:19

Read: Matthew 6:5–15

JESUS' FOLLOWERS didn't follow him long before they realized that prayer was important and normal for him. Luke 5:16 says this, "But Jesus often withdrew to lonely places and prayed." As a follower of Jesus, it will become normal for you to pray as well. In this passage, Jesus is contrasting good prayer and bad prayer.

What is the difference between good and bad prayer?

....

....

....

In Matthew 6:9–13, Jesus teaches his followers how to pray. The Lord's Prayer is not intended to be a rote prayer that is prayed over and over but rather is an example of how to pray. Think about prayer more as a conversation between two friends, not a formula. You can talk with God about anything. Feel free to use your own words to express your thoughts and concerns to God. Notice the components of this simple prayer:

→ **Relationship**—"Our Father in heaven" teaches us that we are in a loving relationship with our Heavenly Father and with others as well who are part of the family.

→ **Respect**—"Hallowed be your name" teaches us that God is holy and as such must receive honor and respect. Tell the Lord how much he means to you and honor him.

→ **Reign**—"Let your kingdom come" teaches us that we start with what God wants. He wants to rule in our hearts. When we pray "let your kingdom come," we are inviting him be our leader and our guide. We bow our lives before him when we pray, "let your kingdom come."

→ **Food**—"Give us today our daily bread" teaches us that we can ask God to meet our basic needs today. When our lives are lined up with his values, we can ask for fuel to do it.

→ **Forgiveness**—"Forgive us our debts as we also have forgiven our debtors" teaches us that when we pray we remember we need forgiveness as much as everyone else. God expects us to model to others the forgiveness he gives to us. In fact, this is so important for us that God requires us to forgive others in order for us to receive his forgiveness. This is important!

→ **Freedom**—"And lead us not into temptation but deliver us from the evil one" teaches us that God can help us be victorious in every temptation. With God's help we can be delivered from the things that are destroying us.

Where does Jesus say his followers should go when we pray? ....
....

It's really important to find a quiet place and a time that you can be alone to pray. There are many ways to do this. You can get up a few minutes earlier than usual, perhaps before others get out of bed. Or, you can go for a walk in the neighborhood.

When and where do you plan to pray? ....
....

You will want to set aside time each day to follow Jesus in prayer. Start with a small amount of time, perhaps five to ten minutes. Eventually, you will probably increase the time but for now set aside at least five minutes. You learn to pray by praying. Feel free to use the six components of the Lord's Prayer to direct your thoughts and words to God. Use your own words to express your thoughts to God. Prayer is not a magic formula. It's just a friend talking with a friend.

As you talk with God, take a few minutes to listen to him as well. Rarely does God speak audibly. In fact, it has never happened to me. But I do have thoughts that come to me occasionally when I pray, and I have learned that's one of the ways he speaks to me. If you think God might be speaking to you, take a moment to write it down and test it out. One good test is whether it is consistent with what God says elsewhere in his Word. God never contradicts himself. You may not yet know whether what you hear is God or not so feel free to share it with your spiritual coach or a pastor to confirm it. You will learn to tell the difference between what God is speaking and what are just your thoughts.

Prayer:
God, it is great to know I am part of your family and that you are my loving heavenly Father. I give you honor.

Truly there is no one like you. I respect you more than I can adequately express with my own words. Please rule my life. Lead me today. Thank you for your provisions for my life. I have everything I really need. Forgive me where I have done wrong. (Go ahead and mention specific things for which you know you need forgiveness.) I choose to extend your forgiveness to everyone around me as well, Lord, because you have been so gracious to me. Lead me away from doing the things I know are destructive and to a path of freedom today. It's great having you in my life. Amen.

Attribute Seven • Overview
Learn to Manage

"Come, follow me," Jesus said, "and I will make you fishers of men." Matthew 4:19

Read: Matthew 6:19–24

W HAT WOULD YOU CONSIDER to be your treasure? For some of us, it is definitely our money. For others, it's reputation. Or time off. Or shoes. Really! I have a box of newspaper clippings of my past sports triumphs. My mom found it when she was moving and shipped it to my house. I opened it up and found that the newspaper clippings were yellow, following apart, and the grand statements of my athletic ability lived only in my head and not on the actual pages. My treasure of newspaper clippings is just stuff. They are not going to last.

Jesus is kind enough and direct enough to address the issue of what we treasure early in our lives as followers. He wants the best for us, and he can't bear for us to waste time and energy on things that simply aren't part of our trip as a follower.

What kinds of things does Jesus say we should not store up? ....

What are some examples of things that moths can eat, rust can destroy, and thieves can steal? ....

What reason does Jesus give for not storing up these things? ....

What kinds of things does Jesus say we should store up?
....

What reason does Jesus give for storing up these things?
....

You must not miss Jesus' statement, "For where your treasure is, there your heart will be also." He does *not* say as many think, "For where your heart is, there your treasure will be also." He says the opposite. In other words, where you put your treasure, that's where your heart will go. Your treasures really are your time, your talent, and your money. He's saying that where you choose to invest your treasure, you will discover your heart will follow. Your heart is submissive to your treasure. He says it blatantly in verse 24, "You cannot serve both God and money." It's impossible to love both. You have to make a choice.

This was a tough one for me early in my walk with Christ. I grew up with this obsession of wanting more money and toys in my life. I picked jobs for my future based on how much money it would bring into my life. I had to surrender my desire to make lots of money when I became a follower of Jesus. You will, too. It's one of the best decisions I have ever made. God supplies everything I need. And it all makes sense based on what we have already learned as a follower. We exist for him and we fulfill our purpose in this life when we use his resources to join what he is doing in the world. The psalmist says it this way in Psalm 24:1, "The earth is the LORD's, and everything in it." That's another way of saying, "It's all God's."

What kinds of things do you treasure that you need to surrender to God?..
....

What are some places or areas of your life in which you need to invest so that your heart goes where you want it to go?..
....
....

What are you going to invest in each of these areas?
....
....
....

Share your decisions with your spiritual coach this week. Ask your spiritual coach how she invests her treasures (time, talent, and money) so that her heart lines up with God's purposes in the world. Also, ask her what has happened as a result of these investments.

> **Prayer:**
> Jesus, thank you for telling me the truth about my treasures. I choose to serve you and not money. Help me to be courageous enough to invest in things that I know will matter to you. Help me to stop investing in things that won't matter one second after I pass from this life. I give this whole area of treasures over to you. I trust you with my life and my treasure. Amen.

Attribute One

•

Learn to Be With Jesus

Attribute One • Introduction
Learn to Be With Jesus

THE MORE TIME YOU SPEND WITH JESUS, the more you will love him and become like him. That's why it is so important to learn how to be with him.

When you first get married, a lot of your life changes as you learn how to be with the other person. Everything is affected—how you do things, when you do things, everything. As a follower of Jesus, you are learning how to make Jesus your first priority. Before you may have just done things without thinking much of him, but now that you realize he is always with you, you may start to view things or do things differently. You are learning to allow him to lead in every area of life and to show you life from his perspective. In this lesson we are going to focus on learning how to enjoy being with him throughout the day regardless of what else is going on.

A logical time to be with him is during a quiet time. We'll talk a little about how to set that up. A quiet devotional time is a good start, but Jesus is with you *always*. As you learn to remain in him, to be with him, he will change everything. He'll show you how to live life to the full in a way that brings God honor. He'll teach you through his Word and in your prayer time how to hear his voice. He'll even show you how to love people and to live a joyful life. Sound good? It is! Serving Jesus is the best life! That's what this lesson is about.

Attribute One • Step One
Learn to Remain in Him

Scripture Memory (new):

[28] "Come to me, all you who are weary and burdened, and I will give you rest. [29] Take my yoke upon you and learn from me, for I am gentle and humble in heart, and you will find rest for your souls. [30] For my yoke is easy and my burden is light." Matthew 11:28–30

Scripture Memory (review): Matthew 4:19

Read: John 15:1–10

HARD WORK HAS BEEN THE BACKBONE of my family heritage. My dad is one of the hardest-working people I know. It has rubbed off on me in a major way. I don't know how to stop working, because I am results-driven. This has plagued me as I have learned to follow Jesus. For example, I sometimes find myself trying to do the work of the ministry on my own and asking for help only if I absolutely have to. That is pride, thinking I can do anything, even God's work, on my own. Good thing that God's Word teaches me otherwise.

John 15 describes how essential it is that we remain in Christ, staying connected to him and dependent on him as our source for life. God has a purpose for each one of our lives. His purpose is that we would fulfill his purpose (bear fruit) in his world. We are not on this planet for ourselves or to find *our* purpose. We are here for him and to fulfill *his* purpose. Jesus uses an analogy of a vine and the fruit it produces to make this point.

Who does Jesus say is the vine? ....

What is the role of the Father? ....

....

What is the role of the follower of Christ? ....

The word "remain" appears eleven times in John 15:1–10, always in reference to staying close to and connected to Jesus. I'll remind us again that following Jesus is always about staying close to Jesus, remaining in him.

What promise does Jesus give us in the first part of John 15:4? ....

....

If you remain in him, he promises to remain in you. Do you want to remain in Christ? There's a great passage in James 4:8 that says something similar: "Come near to God and he will come near to you." When you reach out to God, he will reach out to you.

One of the ways you can reach out to God and grow closer to him is through worship. To "worship" God simply means you choose to put your life in service for him. You declare to God that he is your final authority and that you want to honor him with your life. Some people find it helpful to sing to God in worship. We express our love, thankfulness, and commitment to God at our services and gatherings. I encourage you to begin to do this right away. There is something powerful that happens when you reach out to God. It is important to know that you can also do this at home. If you need help with this, talk with your spiritual coach about it. He or she should be able to help you.

Based on John 15:1–4, why can't a follower of Jesus be a "rugged individualist?" ....

....

We are going to explore some of the ways we can learn to remain in him in the following days, but right now you may realize, as I do, that you need to repent for trying to live life on your own without God. Why not take a few minutes right now to just enjoy your connection to Christ.

Prayer:

Dear Jesus, thank you for the invitation to follow you. It is amazing to me that you want me to remain close to you forever. I am humbled that you, the Creator of the universe, would love me and desire to be close to me and me to you. I declare that you are the final authority in my life and that I want to honor you with my life. Forgive me for trying to do life on my own. I turn away from trying to do life my own way and I turn to you. I accept your invitation to remain in you and your promise to remain in me. I realize that I cannot bear the kind of fruit that you have planned for my life on my own. I am here for you. Amen.

Thought for the Day:

Write out the following words "I am in you" on an index card. Look at the card throughout the day and allow your awareness of God's presence in you to affect how you do your work and life.

Attribute One • Step Two
Learn to Recognize Fruit

Scripture Memory:

28 "Come to —, all you who are —— and burdened, and I will give you ___ . 29 Take my ___ upon you and learn from___, for I am gentle and _____ in heart, and you will find rest for your___. 30 For my ___ is easy and my burden is___ ." ————————11:28–30

28 "Come to me, all you who are weary and burdened, and I will give you rest. 29 Take my yoke upon you and learn from me, for I am gentle and humble in heart, and you will find rest for your souls. 30 For my yoke is easy and my burden is light." Matthew 11:28–30

Read: John 15:5–6; Galatians 5:22–23

I LOVE TRAVELING TO NEW COUNTRIES. One of the things I love about new countries is trying all the fruits from that country. Bananas in St. Lucia. Mangos in Costa Rica. Grapes in Italy. Watermelon in the United States!

Who does Jesus say is the vine?..

What are we?...

....

Why do you think Jesus wants us to stay connected with the Father?...

....

Jesus says in John 15:5, "If a man remains in me and I in him, he will bear much fruit." In other words, if you stay close to God, you will bear much fruit that looks like God. Furthermore, you cannot bear godly fruit on your own. I will put it another way. If you go to an apple tree, what do you expect? If you go to a grape vine, what do you expect? The same applies to God. If you stay connected to God, what can you expect? God has summarized what his fruit is like in Galatians 5:22–23.

The fruit of the Spirit is:

+ **Love**—loving people without expecting anything back, no strings attached

+ **Joy**—delight, being in a good mood because God is exceptionally good or satisfying

+ **Peace**—health and wholeness in relationships and personal well being

+ **Patience**—prolonged restraint of anger and agitation

+ **Kindness**—friendly, regardless of how people treat you

+ **Goodness**—being generous and kind to people

+ **Faithfulness**—confident trust in God that results in consistent actions

+ **Gentleness**—humility, considerateness, meekness, preferring others

+ **Self-control**—disciplined, control over actions and appetites

We need all of them, don't we?
Which of these do you need the most right now?............

What would change if God would give you that fruit?...

....

Make whatever you mentioned above a matter of prayer. Ask God to give you his fruit in your life. When you remain in Christ, you and others will begin to see God's fruit in your life. Isn't he awesome? Like any fruit, it takes time to grow. Don't become impatient with yourself when it doesn't happen overnight. Just stay close to Jesus, delighting in him and in his Word. Trust him. When you notice some fruit, thank him for it. Enjoy the changes he is bringing about in your life.

The latter part of John 15:5 reminds us that becoming like Christ is not something we do on our own or by our own efforts. Notice that it says clearly, "Apart from me you can do nothing." Wow! So much for trying to produce godly fruit on your own! Can't do it! Don't even try it without the Lord.

Prayer:
Heavenly Father, thank you for the assurance that you are my source and that you will produce fruit in my life as I remain in you. I look forward to it. I pray that nothing in my life will inhibit your fruit from growing in me. I don't want to grow fruit so that people will look at me. I want to grow it so that people will look to you and so that you will receive the glory. Change me into your likeness, I pray. Amen.

Attribute One • Step Three
Learn to Be With Him as You Read Scripture

1.3

Scripture Memory:

^{28} "Come to ___, all ___ who are ___ ___ ___, and I will ___ ___ ___. ^{29} Take my ___ ___ ___ and learn ___ ___, for I am ___ ___ ___ ___ ___, and you will ___ ___ ___ ___ ___. ^{30} For my ___ ___ ___ and my ___ ___ ___." ___ ___:28–30

^{28} *"Come to me, all you who are weary and burdened, and I will give you rest. ^{29} Take my yoke upon you and learn from me, for I am gentle and humble in heart, and you will find rest for your souls. ^{30} For my yoke is easy and my burden is light." Matthew 11:28–30*

Read: John 15:7; John 1:1–18; Psalm 1

NOTICE JOHN 15:7, "IF YOU REMAIN IN ME and my words remain in you...." Part of remaining in him is that his words need to remain in us. Earlier in this Gospel, in John 1:1–4, the writer describes Jesus this way:

> In the beginning was the Word, and the Word was with God, and the Word was God. He was with God in the beginning. Through him all things were made; without him nothing was made that has been made. In him was life, and that life was the light of men.

Then, John 1:14a states, "The Word became flesh and made his dwelling among us." The point is this: Jesus is the exact representation of what God is like. When you want to know what God is like, look at Jesus.

In order to really look at Jesus, you are going to have to read and review often the four books of the Bible that tell you specifically about Jesus (Matthew, Mark, Luke, and John). In these books, you learn how he thinks and acts in various situations.

The rest of the New Testament (Acts through Revelation) tells you how Jesus continued and continues to lead and direct his followers (the church) since his death and resurrection. But it doesn't stop there. Jesus also said that the rest of the Bible points to him as well: "Everything must be fulfilled that is written about me in the Law of Moses, the Prophets and the Psalms" (Luke 24:44). As a follower of Jesus, you will want to eventually read and study the entire Bible so you can allow his words to remain in you.

The idea of reading and studying the whole Bible may seem like a huge task right now. Don't let it overwhelm you. Just read a little bit each day and apply it to your life. As you begin to develop your quiet time with God, I recommend you do the following:

- Set a regular time and a place. It should be a quiet and a private place. Remember Jesus' words in Matthew 6:6: "But when you pray, go into your room, close the door and pray to your Father, who is unseen. Then your Father, who sees what is done in secret, will reward you." I like the evening because it helps me dwell on good things before bed. Some prefer the morning. The important thing is that you make regular time for God. What time and place works best for you?

- Decide on a Bible reading plan.
  - Read straight through an entire book of the Bible, one at a time, at your own pace. I encourage you to start with the Gospel of Matthew since that is our primary textbook.

- ✦ Don't read so much that you cannot reflect on its meaning. Many people start with a chapter a day.[1]
- ✦ Don't jump around as you read, reading a few verses here and there in that book or another book. You will be better able to understand what you are reading if you read it in context.

- Pray for guidance before you start reading. Ask Jesus to guide you into truth through his Word. Remember, he is with you.

- Make notes of what you notice and what you think God may be speaking to you as you read. A small notebook in which to write these things is helpful. I like to underline verses that stand out to me and write in the margins of my Bible. I highly recommend you do something similar.

- Prayerfully respond to what you are reading. If you notice something in your life needs to change, pray that God will help you change it. If you notice an aspect of God that is encouraging, thank God for it. If an action is needed, ask God for wisdom in how to carry out the action.

- Remember your focus is on Jesus and not the habit of having a quiet time.

Prayer:
Dear Jesus, thank you for providing a way for me to remain in you through your Word. Open my mind to your thoughts and your ways and your ideas. Teach me how to remain in your words so you can bear your fruit through me. Help me to set aside a specific time each day at _____ to meet with you and to read your Word. I rest in your guidance. Amen.

Attribute One • Step Four
Learn to Be With Christ in Prayer

Scripture Memory:

²⁸ "Come ___ ___, all ___ ___ ___ ___ ___ ___, and
I ___ ___ ___ ___. ²⁹ Take ___ ___ ___ ___ ___ ___
___ ___, for ___ ___ ___ ___ ___ ___ ___, and you
___ ___ ___ ___ ___. ³⁰ For ___ ___ ___ ___ ___
___ ___ ___ ___." ___ ___ ___ ___ ___:___–___

---

²⁸ *"Come to me, all you who are weary and burdened, and I will
give you rest. ²⁹ Take my yoke upon you and learn from me, for
I am gentle and humble in heart, and you will find rest for your
souls. ³⁰ For my yoke is easy and my burden is light." Matthew
11:28–30*

Read: John 15:7; Matthew 7:7–12; James 4:2–3

IN THE PREVIOUS STEP, WE FOCUSED on the first half
of John 15:7 that reminded us of the importance of
remaining connected with God. In this step, we are focusing
on the effect this has on our prayer life: "If you remain in me
and my words remain in you, ask whatever you wish, and it
will be given you."

When you remain in Jesus and remain in his Word, you
will learn to pray his kind of prayers, and God will answer
them. Prayer is not like a magic genie. It is not about saying
the right words and "presto," getting your wish. The Lord

does not give you everything you want or everything you ask for.

What does James 4:2–3 say are the reasons why some prayers are not answered? ....
....

The invitation is to get close to Jesus so you know the things about which he cares most. When you align your heart with his desires, there is an open-endedness about what can happen in prayer. God values your creativity. He says that if you remain in him and in his Word, then you can ask him for what is in your heart. I think Jesus would say, "If you will pray as I please, then you can pray as you please." There is a whole world of discovery between you and God. Stay close to him and start asking him for great things for his kingdom. He just might say, "Great idea!" and make it happen.

It is important to know that God answers your prayers. Sometimes God says "Yes" by saying "No." And sometimes he is a little late, but always on time. But God is always good and it should never be said of you that you don't have because you simply did not ask.

In Matthew 7:7–11, Jesus says something similar:

> Ask and it will be given to you; seek and you will find; knock and the door will be opened to you. For everyone who asks receives; he who seeks finds; and to him who knocks, the door will be opened. Which of you, if his son asks for bread, will give him a stone? Or if he asks for a fish, will give him a snake? If you, then, though you are evil, know how to give good gifts to your children, how much more will your Father in heaven give good gifts to those who ask him!

In short, stay close to the Lord to learn his heart. Pray Jesus' kind of prayers and you can count on your good heavenly Father to answer them.

I have talked with some people who think they should pray only when they absolutely have to, as if you only get so many answered prayers in your life so you had better save them for when you really need them. That is not how God is! He tells us to ask. That's not my idea. Those are his words. Ask! Just ask!

All this talk about asking makes me want to talk with God right now. Got anything on your mind you would like him to answer? Why not talk with him about it? I have modeled some of my prayers up to this point. It's time for you to fly solo a little bit. I'll help you with suggestions.

Prayer:
1. Talk with God like you would a good friend.
2. Thank God for what he is doing in your life right now.
3. If something about this lesson stood out to you, talk with him about it.
4. Ask God in your own words for the things that are on your mind and then tell him that you will trust him.

Attribute One • Step Five
Learn How Remaining in Christ Affects Others

Scripture Memory:

28 "_____ ___ ___, ___ ___ ___ _____ _____ _____ _____, ___
29
__ ___ _____ . _____ ___ ____ ____ ___ ____ ____

_____ __, ___ __ __ _____ ___ _____ __ _____, ___ _____
30
____ ___ _____ . _____ __ ___ ____ ____
_____ __ ___ . " _____ ___:__-__

28 "Come to me, all you who are weary and burdened, and I will give you rest. 29 Take my yoke upon you and learn from me, for I am gentle and humble in heart, and you will find rest for your souls. 30 For my yoke is easy and my burden is light." Matthew 11:28–30

Read: John 15:9–12

I WISH IT WEREN'T TRUE but there are some people who claim to be followers of Christ who are simply awful to be around. They are flat-out negative. They seem to have the attitude that serving the Lord is a burden they have to bear. They have made a decision to get through it, kind of like you get through a root canal. I don't know what Bible they are reading, but that's not what Jesus had in mind for his followers, as this passage attests.

First, Jesus reminds us of how much he loves us, "As the Father has loved me, so have I loved you." We see glimpses of the Father's love for his Son, Jesus, throughout the Scriptures. At Jesus' baptism, the Father affirms his love for the Son. He says, "This is my Son, whom I love; with him I am well pleased" (Matthew 3:17). Then, when Jesus was momentarily changed on the mountain, the Father again declares his love for Jesus, "This is my Son, whom I love; with him I am well pleased. Listen to him!" (Matthew 17:5). In Jesus' prayer right before he died, several times he mentions God's amazing love for him, "I have made you known to them, and will continue to make you known in order that the love you have for me may be in them and that I myself may be in them" (John 17:26). Jesus said simply that the love he received from the Father, he has given to us. He just calls us to remain in that love. Then, Jesus tells us how to remain in his love.

How do we remain in his love according to verse 10?
....
....

According to verse 12, what is his command?................
....

This is the part that my friends who are not enjoying Jesus don't get. It's not a huge burden to give away something so wonderful as the love of Jesus.

Did someone ever give you a special gift? Perhaps it was tickets to a special athletic event or a great vacation that you couldn't afford. Perhaps someone gave his time when you needed it the most. I can think of lots of these, but one stands out to me right now. I was going through a difficult struggle right after I graduated from high school. My soon-to-be mother-in-law invited me to go on a vacation with her and her family to Yellowstone. I don't remember paying for a single thing, but it wasn't about the money for the vacation; it was about being invited into her family and her life. I felt so welcomed, loved and at home. It really helped me get through a tough time in my life to feel that kind of acceptance and love. Here's my point: after I got through that time, I thought about how caring my mother-in-law was, and it made me want to be like that for others. I want to do for others what I experienced. It's not a big burden, because I know what being cared for feels like.

That's all Jesus is saying in this passage. Just give away the love you are experiencing from him. It's not a burden. In fact, it is just the opposite. It's fun. It brings you joy. Jesus says in verse 11, "I have told you this so that my joy may be in you and that your joy may be complete." His command is just that we would love others like he has loved us. Remaining in Christ's love will cause you to want to give his love away to others. The more you receive from him, the more you are going to want to give away.

Sometimes my heart goes out to "Christians" who are not having fun following Jesus. I wonder if they have ever stayed in Christ's presence long enough to experience his extravagant love. Let that never be said of you. You now know the secret of the joyful Christian life. Stay close to Jesus and give away what he gives to you. He will change the world around you if you will do that.

Prayer:
Draw me close to you, Jesus. Thank you for your amazing love and friendship. Help me to give away to others what you have given to me so the world will know you are real and that you love them.

Attribute One
Decisions

Attribute Two
•
Learn to Listen

Attribute Two • Introduction
Learn to Listen

IT IS SIGNIFICANT THAT THE FIRST THING Jesus did after calling his disciples to follow him was to invite them to listen and watch as he taught in the synagogues and healed people (Matthew 4:23–25). I probably would have expected him to take some time to build a relationship and to teach them privately. Not Jesus. He took them right into the middle of real ministry where they could hear his words and see them put into practice right away.

As you are learning to listen to Jesus, it is important to know he will speak to you in four ways: through his written Word (the Bible); through prayer; in circumstances; and through his people, the church.

Furthermore, hearing Jesus' words is not enough. You need to *do* what he says. Matthew 7:24–25 records Jesus words:

> Therefore everyone who *hears* these words of mine and *puts them into practice* is like a wise man who built his house on the rock. The rain came down, the streams rose, and the winds blew and beat against that house; yet it did not fall, because it had its foundation on the rock. [Emphasis mine.]

As a follower of Jesus, you will want to be in settings where you can hear the teachings of Jesus and see him change lives. Acts 2:46 describes the earliest followers of Jesus meeting regularly in large gatherings (the temple courts) and in small groups (homes). We need both. That's why we have both large groups (worship services and gatherings) and house churches or small groups. At our services and gatherings, we worship God, hear his Word taught, and serve others. It's also a great place to bring a friend who wants to see what following Christ is all about. In our house churches and small groups, we ask questions, encourage one another, and learn how to hear and apply God's Word to our daily lives. We also have Jesus' assurance that he is with us in a special way, "For where two or three come together in my name, there am I with them" (Matthew 18:20). In both size groups, however, it is really important to focus on learning to hear the words of Jesus so you can put them into practice.

Besides a large service and a small group, it is also important to learn to hear Jesus by reading the Bible. One of the challenges that you can encounter is thinking you already know the Bible. If you were raised in a home where the Bible was read or taught, you can sometimes rely on the cognitive information you retained instead of getting to really know Jesus on a personal level.

In this lesson we are going to focus on learning to carefully hear the words of Jesus in the Scriptures so you can put them into practice. Besides attending a corporate worship service and a small group, I am encouraging you to set aside at least fifteen minutes each day for "hearing" time. As you learn to hear the Word of God, you need to develop the habit of "doing" it right way. There should not be a lengthy time between "hearing" and "doing." Jesus expects you to act on what you know. You don't need to learn a lot each day, just enough so you can apply it to your life that day.

We'll talk more about this throughout the lesson, but I would like to give you some advice:

⁕ Choose a Bible reading plan that works for you. I suggest reading the passages in this guide as your reading for now. You may want to read the entire book of Matthew when you are done. After that you might want to work your way through the New

Testament. The important thing is that you make Bible reading a normal part of your day.

+ Pray before you start reading. Ask God to point out things to you. Don't rush through your Bible reading. Read with an open heart.

+ When something stands out to you, underline it in your Bible. It is easy to go back and review if it is marked in some way.

+ Write down what stood out to you. I use a journal to record these observations. After writing out what stood out to me in the passage, I usually write out how it applies to me and to my life right now. I am amazed how God speaks to my situations through the Bible.

+ Pray. Ask God how he wants you to act on what stood out to you that day. Some days you will have something significant to apply. At other times, you will have something to think about. The important thing is that you read and apply it right away.

You may want to reflect with your coach about how your devotional time is going. Don't give up on the process if you are struggling with consistency. Developing a new habit takes time and effort. Most people say it takes twenty-one days to make a new habit. Stay with it. Just do it. I believe you will find God's Word to have a powerful influence on your life if you will develop the habit of learning to listen.

When will you do your Bible reading and "listening" time?...
....

Are you involved in a small group? If so, how is it going?
....

Prayer:

Lord, help me to learn to listen to your words so I can apply them to the life you have given me. I want to build a foundation that will last when the storms of life come. I want you to be the cornerstone of my life from this day onward. Help me to faithfully apply your Word to my life. Help me to be a doer of your Word and not just a hearer. I ask this in Jesus' name, amen.

Attribute Two • Step One
Learn to Be Happy

Scripture Memory (new):

²⁴ "Therefore everyone who hears these words of mine and puts them into practice is like a wise man who built his house on the rock. ²⁵ The rain came down, the streams rose, and the winds blew and beat against that house; yet it did not fall, because it had its foundation on the rock." Matthew 7:24–25

Scripture Memory (review):   Matthew 4:19
                                 Matthew 11:28–30

Read: Matthew 5:1–12

WHAT WORDS ARE REPEATED in Matthew 5:1–12?.........
....

Each of the nine statements in this section begins with Jesus saying, "Blessed." Some translators actually translate the word *blessed* as "happy." This is not a bad translation, but the English word *happy* is too shallow for what the word means. I'll do my best to explain what *blessed* means below.

> In secular Greece the island of Cyprus was called the blest island. The idea was that those who lived in Cyprus never had to leave its shores in order to have all they needed to be content...the island was self-contained. No one had to search for the needs and wants of life.[1]

That's partly what *blessed* means—when you have it, you

are fortunate and satisfied and you don't have to look elsewhere for it.

The Old Testament meaning of *blessed* meant you were approved by God. In other words, you can't be a blessed person and not be approved by God. "When we are blessed by God, our happiness does not come from circumstances, or by accident, or through a diligent search. It comes because we stand approved before the Creator of the universe."[2]

According to these verses, who is blessed?......................

....

Does anything surprise you about those who are blessed?

....

....

In these verses, Jesus teaches us the truth, not as our world teaches, but something we would never discover on our own. He teaches that blessing is not linked to how much you have in this world. Blessed people are those who realize they have nothing to bring to God, the poor in spirit. If you discover that truth, regardless of your economic reality, you literally will receive it all—the kingdom of heaven, the mother lode of all gifts. Blessing is for everyone who knows the truth about what he or she has before God. We have nothing to offer him except our lives and he has everything to offer us. These verses illustrate how important it is to come to Christ to learn from him what life, blessing, and everything else in life is all about.

What kinds of things do you tend to rely on to find your sense of worth and value?......................................

....

How might your life be different if you found all of your significance and value in God?..............................

....

....

With these verses Jesus offers blessing and hope for every

person on the planet. For those who are mourning, he promises comfort. For those who prefer others ahead of themselves (the meek), he promises a huge inheritance. For those who are hungry and thirsty to do right things (righteousness), he promises they will be satisfied. For those who are merciful, he promises mercy. For those who are pure in heart, he promises an audience with God. For those who seek peace, he promises to call them his family. For those who are persecuted in this life, he promises that God's kingdom belongs to them. They get it all. For those who are insulted and spoken against, Jesus says they can rejoice because they are in great company; that's what happened to the prophets and eventually to Jesus as well. You simply cannot lose when you find everything in God.

Take a few moments to think about how you have nothing except your life to offer God. You may even want to close your eyes and turn your open palms upward as a symbol of your poverty of spirit. Now talk with God about that.

Prayer:
Heavenly Father, I realize I have nothing to offer you except my life. Although it is broken and messed up, it is all I have. If you can do something with it, please take it. I realize I am poor in spirit but you say that I am blessed because of that. That's very encouraging to me. It gives me hope. The ground is level before you. I come to you the same as every other person under your leadership comes: empty-handed. You give me everything. I receive your kingdom in my life. You are so good. Have your way in my life.

Attribute Two • Step Two
Learn to Go to the Source

Scripture Memory:

[24] "Therefore _____ who hears these _____ of mine and puts them into _____ is like a _____ man who built his _____ on the rock. [25] The _____ came down, the streams ___, and the winds blew and _____ against that house; yet it did not ____, because it had its _____ on the rock." _____ 7:24–25

[24] *"Therefore everyone who hears these words of mine and puts them into practice is like a wise man who built his house on the rock. [25] The rain came down, the streams rose, and the winds blew and beat against that house; yet it did not fall, because it had its foundation on the rock." Matthew 7:24–25*

Read: 2 Timothy 3:16–17

READING THE BIBLE WILL BE AN IMPORTANT PART of your growth as a follower of Christ. 2 Timothy 3:16–17 describes what makes the Bible so important and the significant role it will have in your life as a follower. What claim does 2 Timothy 3:16 make? ....

....

"God-breathed" means "inspired by God." It means that God communicated his message through the thoughts and vocabulary of the human writers. It doesn't mean he "dictated" it, but it does mean that God directed the writer even in the selection of his words so that God's intent and purpose come through. It's amazing to realize that God has given us in writing his thoughts in human language. Pretty cool.

In what four ways does this passage say that the Bible can help you? Write them below.

....

....

If you wrote teaching, rebuking, correcting and training in righteousness, you are correct. The Bible will help you learn information about God and how to follow Christ (teaching). It will help you discover things you are doing that you need to do differently (rebuking). It will help you restore and reestablish your foundation so you can be who you were designed to be (correcting). And, it will help train and discipline you to honor God with your life and actions (training in righteousness). Isn't it great that you can know where to find the answers to those life questions?

What is your plan to incorporate Bible reading into your life? Share this with your spiritual coach when you get together...

....

Do you have specific questions about God for which you could use an answer? Your spiritual coach may or may not know the answers, but one of the leaders of the church will help steer you in the right direction. What are your questions?..

....

....

Do you have questions about what it means to be a follower of Jesus? What are they?...

....

....

Are there things you are doing in your life that you are aware need God's help to change now that you are a follower of Jesus? ....

....

....

Do you feel you need restoration in a certain area of your life so you can build a solid foundation with God? ....

....

God is in the process of changing your life and mine. He loves you with an everlasting love. There is nothing you can do to make God love you more or make him love you less. But God loves you too much to leave you where you are. He wants you to become all that he has designed you to become. For that to happen, he needs to change you. There is your work and there is his work. Your work is to ask God and to submit yourself to him. It is God's will to change you into his likeness. That will happen as you systematically put yourself in a situation to hear God's Word and to put it into practice. Call to mind again Jesus' words in Matthew 7:24–25:

> Therefore everyone who hears these words of mine and puts them into practice is like a wise man who built his house on the rock. The rain came down, the streams rose, and the winds blew and beat against that house; yet it did not fall, because it had its foundation on the rock.

What decision(s) are you making today? ....

....

Prayer:

Heavenly Father, thank you for your Word that guides me into truth. Help me to make the Scriptures part of my everyday life. With your help, I am going to attempt to read the Bible each day. I need to know your thoughts so I can know how to please you and live the life you have designed me to live. I ask for your help with this. I want to please you. Amen.

Attribute Two • Step Three
Learn to See Jesus in Scripture

Scripture Memory:

²⁴ "Therefore _____ who_____ these_____ of mine and
_____ them into _____ is like a _____ man who_____ his
_____ on the _____. ²⁵ The _____ _____ _____ , the streams
____ , and the_____ _____ and _____against that house; yet
it____ ____ ____, because it had its _____ on the _____ ."
_____ __:24–25

²⁴ *"Therefore everyone who hears these words of mine and puts*
them into practice is like a wise man who built his house on the
rock. ²⁵ The rain came down, the streams rose, and the winds
blew and beat against that house; yet it did not fall, because it
had its foundation on the rock." Matthew 7:24–25

Read: Luke 24:13–49

WHAT STANDS OUT TO YOU about these accounts?.........
....

After Jesus' resurrection from the dead he appeared to
his disciples. Jesus said something very interesting in Luke
24:44, "Everything must be fulfilled that is written about me
in the Law of Moses, the Prophets and the Psalms." Verse 45
says, "Then he opened their minds so they could understand
the Scriptures." At least two things are important about this.
First, Jesus pointed his followers to read the Scriptures to

understand who he was. Second, Jesus helped them understand by opening their minds. Both are true for you and other followers of Jesus.

It might be helpful to learn some basic things about the Bible. Open your Bible to the front cover and turn each page until you find what looks like a table of contents. You will notice that the Bible is made up of two parts: the Old Testament and the New Testament. The Old Testament was written down and took place before the life of Jesus. The New Testament was written by his followers after Jesus' resurrection.

The Old Testament is made up of five main parts: the Pentateuch which is the first five books of the Bible (Genesis through Deuteronomy), the Historical Books (Joshua through Esther), Psalms and Wisdom Literature (Job through Song of Songs), the Major Prophets (Isaiah, Jeremiah, and Ezekiel) and the Minor Prophets (Lamentations and Daniel through Malachi).

The New Testament is made up five main parts as well: Gospels (Matthew through John), Acts, Pauline Epistles (Romans through Philemon), General Epistles (Hebrews through Jude), and Revelation.

Jesus said in essence, "All Scripture points to me." This is helpful for us because anytime you are reading a passage of the Bible, even if it is perhaps confusing, you can ask, "How does this point to Jesus?" And you will be asking the right question.

The writer of Hebrews said this about Jesus: "The Son is the radiance of God's glory and the exact representation of his being, sustaining all things by his powerful word" (Hebrews 1:3).

Jesus came to change our lives. When we read the Bible under his direction, he lovingly and strongly guides us into a new way of life.

Prayer

As we conclude today, rather than praying my prayer, I want to pray over you the prayer the Apostle Paul prayed for the new followers of Jesus in Colossians 1:9–18:

[9] For this reason, since the day we heard about you, we have not stopped praying for you and asking God to fill you with the knowledge of his will through all spiritual wisdom and understanding. [10] And we pray this in order that you may live a life worthy of the Lord and may please him in every way: bearing fruit in every good work, growing in the knowledge of God, [11] being strengthened with all power according to his glorious might so that you may have great endurance and patience, and joyfully [12] giving thanks to the Father, who has qualified you to share in the inheritance of the saints in the kingdom of light. [13] For he has rescued us from the dominion of darkness and brought us into the kingdom of the Son he loves, [14] in whom we have redemption, the forgiveness of sins. [15] He is the image of the invisible God, the firstborn over all creation. [16] For by him all things were created: things in heaven and on earth, visible and invisible, whether thrones or powers or rulers or authorities; all things were created by him and for him. [17] He is before all things, and in him all things hold together. [18] And he is the head of the body, the church; he is the beginning and the firstborn from among the dead, so that in everything he might have the supremacy.

I look forward to hearing the stories of how God changes your life through the power of his Word.

Attribute Two • Step Four
Learn to Overcome Temptation

Scripture Memory:

²⁴ "Therefore _____ ___ _____ these _____ of _____ and
___ ____ into _____ is like a ____ ___ who ____ his
_____ on the ___. ²⁵ The ____ ___ _____ , the _____
____, and the _____ _____ and _____ against that _____; yet
it___ _____, because __ __ __ _____ on the ___."
Matthew 7:__ – __

---

²⁴ *"Therefore everyone who hears these words of mine and puts
them into practice is like a wise man who built his house on the
rock.* ²⁵ *The rain came down, the streams rose, and the winds
blew and beat against that house; yet it did not fall, because it
had its foundation on the rock." Matthew 7:24–25*

Read: Matthew 4:1–11

I FIND IT VERY ENCOURAGING that Jesus doesn't just talk
about what people ought to do. He shows us how to live
and then tells us to do the same. In Matthew 4, Jesus was led
by the Spirit into the desert to be tempted by the devil. Do
you want to know how to handle temptation? Do you want
to know how to succeed every time when you are tempted?
Take note of Jesus.

Jesus was tempted in three ways. According to Matthew
4:2–3, about what was the first temptation? ....

Can you think of some ways you are tempted by normal human appetites?.......................

How did Jesus overcome this temptation?.....................

If your Bible has references, you will see a note to let you know Jesus quoted Deuteronomy 8:3. When Jesus was tempted to use divine power to meet his own physical needs, he remembered the biblical principle that God is responsible for sustaining us by his Word. We exist because God said it. We are here by God and for God and not the other way around. We must submit even our human appetites to God. He will meet them in his way and at his time. It is all a gift from him. Jesus knew this principle because he knew the Word of God. It was in his heart and mind so he did not sin when tempted to do his own thing.

According to Matthew 4:5–6, what did the devil tempt Jesus to do?.......................

By what means did the devil try to convince Jesus he should do this?.......................

Isn't it amazing that the devil even used Scripture on Jesus? The devil knows how powerful Scripture is, but he did something that you should see. He quoted Scripture to make it say what he wanted it to say rather than what God intended it to mean. He cleverly quoted a portion of Psalm 91 out of context, "For he will command his angels concerning you to guard you…they will lift you up in their hands, so that you will not strike your foot against a stone" (vv. 11–12). In context, however, Psalm 91:9 states, "If you make the Most High your dwelling…then no harm will befall you." God's protection comes when we live for him, not when we do foolish things. Be careful to read Scripture for what it says, not what you want it to say.

Notice again that Jesus quoted Scripture to respond to the devil's temptation. See if you can find in the marginal reference in your Bible which passage Jesus quoted.[1] Jesus was tempted to prove he was the Son of God by doing a spectacular sign. God never shows off. Asking God to do that is way out of line. Jesus knew that, because he knew the Word of God, and he could quote it when tempted. You can do the same as you learn God's Word.

What was the main topic of the devil's third temptation for Jesus according to Matthew 4:8–9? ....

Jesus knew he had to suffer and die a cruel death in order to save the whole world. All he had to do was bow down one time to the devil, and he could have the glory without the cross. There are no shortcuts to the will of God. Jesus knew that because he knew the Word of God. We were created to worship only God. I wanted to use these examples because we find in them our example for how to handle temptation. We need to know the truth of God's Word in context so we can apply it to our lives.

There are no shortcuts to following Jesus and to being able to handle temptations when they come. You need to know the truth of God's Word in context. You need daily infusions of God's Word to be able to live the life God has for you. How is your Bible reading going? ....

Prayer:
Heavenly Father, thank you for your Word that teaches me how to live and to overcome temptation. I would not be able to know you personally if it were not for Jesus Christ. His example and your Word in context shows what you are like and what you think. Thank you for sending both to me to show me the way back to you. Help me to prioritize reading and applying your Word to my life daily. Amen.

Attribute Two • Step Five
Learn to Be Productive

Scripture Memory:

24 " _____ ___ ___ ___ ___ ___ ___ __

___ ___ ___ ___ ___ ___ ___ ___ ___

___ __ ___ ___ . 25 ___ ___ ___ ___ ___ , __ ___

__ , ___ ___ ___ ___ ___ ___ ___ ___ ; __

___ ___ ___ , ___ ___ ___ ___ ___ ___ . "

___ __ : __ - __

---

24 *"Therefore everyone who hears these words of mine and puts them into practice is like a wise man who built his house on the rock.* 25 *The rain came down, the streams rose, and the winds blew and beat against that house; yet it did not fall, because it had its foundation on the rock." Matthew 7:24–25*

Read: Luke 8:5–15

IT TAKES TWO HANDS TO COUNT the number of times I have tried to start a garden. I dreamt of vine-ripened tomatoes, fresh squash, and watermelon. I either have the worst soil in the world or no gardening skills. I think it is the soil.

There are several keys to a productive garden. You need the right seeds or starter plants, the right amount of water and sun, protection from pests, and good soil. Many people know about the first three but fail to make sure the soil is prepared properly. It is amazing how much more can be produced if you prepare the soil properly before you plant.

Jesus taught in Luke 8 how the soil of our hearts makes all the difference in our productivity as his followers. What four types of soil did Jesus describe?............................

....

....

He taught about four kinds of heart soils: hard ground, rocky soil, thorny soil, and good soil. Each soil receives the same seed, has the same amount of water and sunlight, and the same exposure to pests, but some never produce at all. Some start to produce but don't make it, some look pretty good but never produce, and others produce greatly. The only difference is the soil.

What does Jesus say is the seed? (Luke 8:11)...................

....

What keeps the soil on the path from producing? (Luke 8:12)...

....

....

What keeps the rocky soil from producing? (Luke 8:13)

....

What keeps the thorny soil from producing? (Luke 8:14)

....

....

What are the characteristics of the person's heart soil that produces greatly? (Luke 8:15)....................................

....

Does the parable of the soil help you identify anything that could keep you from being productive in your walk with Jesus? If so, what is it and what would you like to do about it?...

....

....

God's word will change your life if you are willing to tend the soil of your heart. One of the biggest challenges that many Americans face is the thorn of materialism. Some sacrifice many things (time, energy, sleep, even relationships) so they can own more material goods or have pleasurable experiences. Jesus says our productivity in the kingdom of God can be choked out by worries, riches, and pleasures. God's plan for your life is that you would be a productive follower of Jesus, that your life would count big time for his kingdom. This would be a great time to tell the Lord that you want to surrender your desires and your resources to him. The One who made you knows how to make your life productive. Wouldn't it be a shame to live your whole life and never fulfill the reason why you are here? Wouldn't it be sad to live your life for things that won't matter five seconds after you die? I don't want to do that. I want to hear my Lord say to me one day, "Well done, good and faithful servant." I'm sure you do as well.

Why don't you take a few minutes right now to write out some things you need to adjust. When you have done that, talk to God about each item. Ask him to show you how to cultivate your heart's soil so you produce a hundredfold for him. . . . .

. . . .

. . . .

. . . .

. . . .

. . . .

. . . .

Talk to your spiritual coach about what you feel God is directing you to change. Ask him how following Jesus has made a difference in his priorities in life. He may have some valuable insights into how to align your life to God's values.

Attribute Two
Decisions

....
....
....
....
....
....
....
....
....
....
....
....
....
....
....
....
....
....
....
....
....
....
....
....
....
....
....
....
....
....
....
....
....
....
....

Attribute Three

•

Learn to Heal

Attribute Three • Introduction
Learn to Heal

THE DAY AFTER my oldest daughter turned a year old, my wife and I loaded up our SUV and headed to Fort Collins, Colorado, to speak at a few churches. Our drive would take us through Wyoming. As we entered Wyoming from Utah, we hit some bad weather and ended up sliding off the side of the road. The problem was there was no side of the road. Our SUV flipped down the mountain side. My life flashed before my eyes. There is a lot more to the story than I have time to get into, but in that moment of thinking my family and I were going to die, I yelled out to Jesus to save us. Our vehicle landed right side up at the bottom of the ravine. After all the craziness of ambulances and police, we ended up at the emergency room. When we got there, the doctor examined my daughter, my wife, and I. He looked perplexed and said, "If the police and paramedics hadn't seen the accident, I wouldn't believe your bodies had been through a trauma of this magnitude."

The doctor was correct. Hours, days and weeks afterward brought no stiffness or soreness.

I told you that story for a couple of reasons. First, you need to know that a rational, twenty-first century human being believes he experienced a miracle. We had experienced a deadly car accident with only a few scratches. The doctor was perplexed at the results. Second, healings sometimes happen immediately and sometimes don't. I do not understand why God heals some immediately, some later, and some never at all. For instance, God did not heal my knee when I tore my medial collateral ligament (MCL), among other things. But the Bible teaches us that God heals and he invites us to ask.

In these sessions, as you read a variety of miracle stories, it is my hope that you will not only be open to God's divine intervention but that your faith would grow. If there is a God and if he is as the Bible describes, then God can suspend natural laws at any time to do the supernatural. Jesus said,

> Ask and it will be given to you; seek and you will find; knock and the door will be opened to you. For everyone who asks receives; he who seeks finds; and to him who knocks, the door will be opened. (Matthew 7:7–8)

Ask.

Prayer:
Heavenly Father, you spoke and the world came into existence out of nothing. You said, "Let there be light," and there was light. That is so far beyond anything I can understand. Show me what's real about healing, and hereafter in my life, I want everything you have for me. Amen.

Attribute Three • Step One
The Importance of Touch

Scripture Memory (new):

⁷ "Ask and it will be given to you; seek and you will find; knock and the door will be opened to you. ⁸ For everyone who asks receives; he who seeks finds; and to him who knocks, the door will be opened." Matthew 7:7–8

Scripture Memory (review):   Matthew 4:19
Matthew 11:28–30   Matthew 7:24–25

Read: Matthew 4:18–22

IT IS SIGNIFICANT THAT THE FIRST THING JESUS DID after calling his disciples to follow him was to invite them to hear him teach about God's kingdom and to watch him heal people. From the beginning of their walk with Jesus, they would know that when Jesus is around, anything is possible. Matthew 4:23–24 reads this way:

> Jesus went throughout Galilee, teaching in their synagogues, preaching the good news of the kingdom, and healing every disease and sickness among the people. News about him spread all over Syria, and people brought to him all who were ill with various diseases, those suffering severe pain, the demon-possessed, those having seizures, and the paralyzed, and he healed them.

How do you think it might have affected the early

disciples to see Jesus healing people?..................................
....

According to a survey conducted by Time Magazine, 69 percent of Americans believe in miracles.[1] Do you believe in miracles? Why or why not?..............................
....

There are many miracles recorded in the Bible, but one moves me emotionally more than the rest. Read Matthew 8:1–4.

Several things move me about this story. First, the man was desperate. There was no known cure for leprosy. They no doubt thought about it much like we think of cancer or HIV. Lepers were required to live outside the community. They also had to communicate they were diseased by how they dressed, and they had to keep to themselves (Leviticus 13:45–46; Numbers 5:1–4). Furthermore, sometimes leprosy was a direct punishment from God (Numbers 12:10; 2 Kings 5:27). The normal person wanted nothing to do with a leper for obvious reasons. Somehow the man in Matthew 8 heard about Jesus. He came and knelt before Jesus and said, "… if you are willing, you can make me clean." The depth of need, the humility, the hope demonstrated, all move me. But I think it is the next thing that moves me the most. "Jesus reached out his hand and touched the man." What? Jesus touched the man with the skin disease? Yes, Jesus touched someone who hadn't been touched in who knows how long, perhaps in years. Jesus' heart broke for one who was alone, an outcast, outside of community; one whose body was riddled with disease. He touched him. That's what God is like. His heart is moved by our brokenness. He knows what we are going through, the visible and the invisible, and he cares. The man was not just another notch in Jesus' healing belt. The man with leprosy was a person with a broken life who needed to be touched by his Creator.

There is one more thing about the story that moves me: the humility of the leprous man. He didn't stay away from Jesus; he was not passive. He did not demand that Jesus heal him. He simply believed Jesus could do it, he knelt before him in humility, and he asked.

This story moves me because I have broken places in my life that I would like Jesus to touch. Some of them are easy to see but others are not. Perhaps you have them as well. While it remains a mystery why some people are healed and others are not, this story shows me what God is like. He sees our brokenness. He cares. And he reaches out and touches us in our diseased state. God is not a distant, impersonal and aloof force in the universe. God is a person who reaches out to us in our need. He knows what we need and he is moved by it.

What comes to your mind when you read this description about Jesus?...
....
....

Do you need Jesus to touch an area in your life? What is it?..
....
....

Take a few minutes to talk with Jesus about it right now.
....

Prayer:
Jesus, when you were on this earth you saw people's need and your heart was moved by their suffering. Right now I bring myself to you like the man in Matthew 8. I cannot demand anything. I present my need before you. (Talk with Jesus now about your need even though he already knows.) Would you stretch out your hand and touch me in my need? I really need to know that you are here and that I am not alone in this. I trust your Word

that says that in all things you work for the good of those who love you (Romans 8:28). I do love you and I ask you to have your way in my life. I rest in you now. Amen.

Receiving Jesus' Touch Through Others

You may decide to share your area that needs healing with your spiritual coach or your house church or small group. We were not designed to suffer alone. Jesus designed us to be in community with others to "rejoice with those who rejoice" and to "mourn with those who mourn" (Romans 12:15), and to help "carry each other's burdens" (Galatians 6:2). Regardless of how we got to where we are, God will help us carry our burdens through his people. He may not remove our consequences. The law of sowing and reaping is part of the laws he set up in the universe. But he will help us. One way he helps us is through his people. It's humbling but it is right and it is good. I think you will like it as well.

Attribute Three • Step Two
Recognize Jesus' Authority

Scripture Memory:

⁷ "Ask and it ___ __ ___ to you; seek and ___ ___ ___ ;
knock and the door ___ __ ___ to you. ⁸ For everyone
who asks _____ ; he who seeks ____ ; and to him who
____ , the door will be _____ ." _____ 7:7–8

---

⁷ *"Ask and it will be given to you; seek and you will find; knock
and the door will be opened to you.* ⁸ *For everyone who asks
receives; he who seeks finds; and to him who knocks, the door
will be opened." Matthew 7:7–8*

Read: Matthew 8:5–13

IN THIS STORY, a Roman military officer who was in charge
of a hundred men came to Jesus in Capernaum to let
Jesus know the officer's servant was paralyzed and in terrible
trouble. Jesus said to him, "I will go and heal him." Several
things about this surprise me. First, the man is not a Jew.
The average Jew hated the Roman occupation and wanted
nothing to do with any Roman citizens, especially the
soldiers. Somehow, the centurion knew Jesus was above all
that, that Jesus cared for everyone, even those who have
professions we disdain. Jesus obviously had a reputation
of caring for everyone. So, this man came to the one who
offered hope.

The second thing that surprises me is that Jesus offered to go and heal the man's servant without being asked. Jesus is proactive with his healing. When he hears a need, he responds. This surprises the centurion. He knows the social separation between Jews and Romans. Jews did not enter the homes of non-Jews because they thought it made them unclean. But Jesus was going to go anyway.

Why? Because people matter to God. God is not constrained by traditions and social rules that separate people from God. Aren't you glad of that? Jesus proactively goes to where the needs are.

Furthermore, the centurion is a man of great faith. The centurion tells Jesus he does not deserve to have Jesus come to his house. Instead, the centurion articulates his understanding of authority and then suggests that Jesus could just "say the word" and heal his servant without coming for a visit. The man's faith astonished Jesus and me as well. The man believed Jesus could heal from long distance.

This is exactly what Jesus did. "Jesus said to the centurion, 'Go! It will be done just as you believed it would.' And his servant was healed at that very hour."

As you are learning about healing, you need to know that Jesus cares about people wherever they are found, that he is proactive, and that he responds to faith. The centurion put himself in a position to receive a miracle by believing that Jesus cared and that he could do it.

What comes to your mind as you think about this story?

How might a person put themselves in a position to receive a miracle?

As you read God's Word and observe how Jesus heals people, your faith in God will grow. Faith is simply believing that Jesus cares and that he can do it. It is confident trust.

Do you believe Jesus can heal now? Why or why not?

....

If you struggle with faith, you are not alone. You might be like Thomas, one of the twelve disciples, who struggled with his faith. After Jesus' resurrection, some of the disciples saw Jesus when Thomas was not around. When Thomas heard about it, he refused to believe. His words are recorded in John 20:25: "Unless I see the nail marks in his hands and put my finger where the nails were, and put my hand into his side, I will not believe it." A week later, Jesus appeared to Thomas. He told Thomas to touch his hands and his side and then he said, "Stop doubting and believe." Jesus wasn't upset that Thomas struggled with his faith. He gave him objective data, but he also knew that Thomas needed to make an informed decision to believe.

You might be like the father who was described in Mark 9:14–32 whose son was being tormented by an evil spirit. When the father brought his son to Jesus, "Jesus said, 'Everything is possible for him who believes.' Immediately the boy's father exclaimed, 'I do believe; help me overcome my unbelief!'" (Mark 9:23–24). You may believe but you may also doubt. Bring all that to the Lord and ask him to help you with it.

Why not take some time right now to talk with the Lord about your needs. While you are at it, ask him for help with your faith as well. He can expand your capacity to have confident trust in him.

Prayer:
Heavenly Father, I am encouraged today that nothing can keep you from caring about my life. You have been reaching out to me my whole life. Even though I did not always respond, you continued to pursue me. I am so grateful for that. I believe you can do anything.

Increase my faith. Replace my doubts with faith. Show yourself to me in unmistakable ways and I will respond. (Take the time right now to present your needs to God. Ask him to heal or meet your need. Then, tell God you trust him with his decision.) Thank you for your unfailing love. I need you in my life today. Amen.

Attribute Three • Step Three
Understand Healing Is God's Idea

Scripture Memory:

⁷ "Ask __ __ __ __ __ to __ ; seek __ __ __ __ ;
knock __ __ __ __ __ __ to __ . ⁸ For __ __
__ asks __ ; he __ __ __ ; __ __ him __
__ , __ __ __ __ __ ." __ __ :7–8

---

⁷ *"Ask and it will be given to you; seek and you will find; knock
and the door will be opened to you.* ⁸ *For everyone who asks
receives; he who seeks finds; and to him who knocks, the door
will be opened." Matthew 7:7–8*

Read: Matthew 8:14–17

THE NEXT MIRACLE JESUS PERFORMED was to heal Peter's
mother-in-law. (Peter's stock with his mother-in-law
had to have gone up.) This healing was also a great move on
Jesus' part because she was then able to wait on everyone.
(Don't get upset. I'm just having some fun.) After that
healing, many people were brought to Jesus to be delivered
and healed. Don't miss the explanation in verse 17: "This was
to fulfill what was spoken through the prophet Isaiah: 'He
took up our infirmities and carried our diseases.'"

This is a direct quote of Isaiah 53. The book of Isaiah
was written about seven hundred years before Jesus was
born. Throughout the book there are hints of a leader who

would come to change the course of history and bring peace. Isaiah 53:4–5 describes a suffering servant who would bring healing:

> Surely he took up our infirmities and carried our sorrows, yet we considered him stricken by God, smitten by him and afflicted. But he was pierced for our transgressions, he was crushed for our iniquities; the punishment that brought us peace was upon him, and by his wounds we are healed.

The early followers of Jesus were Jewish. They knew about this prophecy, and they rightly linked its fulfillment to Jesus. Isaiah 53 also describes the suffering servant pouring out his life unto death, bearing the sin of many, and interceding for people who are far from God. These were also fulfilled in Jesus.

I'm telling you all this because I want you to see that it is in the nature of God to heal and restore people. It is God's idea, not ours, that healing takes place. The One who spoke the world into existence can say the word and bring healing to your life.

God still heals bodies and does miracles, but the greatest miracle that will ever take place in your life is God healing your soul. Quoting from Isaiah 53:9, the Apostle Peter explains this in 1 Peter 2:22: "He committed no sin, and no deceit was found in his mouth." He then provided the following explanation in verses 23–25:

> When they hurled their insults at him, he did not retaliate; when he suffered, he made no threats. Instead, he entrusted himself to him who judges justly. He himself bore our sins in his body on the tree, so that we might die to sins and live for righteousness; by his wounds you have been healed. For you were like sheep going astray, but now you have returned to the Shepherd and Overseer of your souls.

We who were once far away from God, can now be close to God because Jesus bore our sins on the cross. Because Jesus did that, God can heal our souls. Why not take a few minutes right now to thank God that Jesus died for your sins and brought healing to your soul. Then, ask him to also heal your body...ask!

> ***Prayer:***
> Heavenly Father, cause my faith to grow. I want to believe you can do anything. Thank you for healing my soul by sending Jesus to bear my sins on the cross. I know I cannot earn your love. Jesus has already earned it for me. I just accept what you did for me and I thank you. Thank you for making me new on the inside. Continue to heal me in every area of my life as well. (Take a few minutes now and tell the Lord about other areas of your life that need his healing touch. Pour out your heart to the Lord and trust him with the results.)

One final thought: healing may or may not come like you expect. But God does all things well. He is with you and you can trust him. He is always good and he is always loving.

Attribute Three • Step Four
Ask in Faith

Scripture Memory:

7 "___ ___ ___ ___ given ___ ___; seek ___ ___ ___ ___ ___;
___ ___ ___ door___ ___ ___ ___ ___ ___ . 8 ___ everyone
___ ___ receives; ___ ___ ___ finds; ___ ___ ___ ___
knocks,___ ___ ___ ___ ___." ___ 7: __–__

7 *"Ask and it will be given to you; seek and you will find; knock and the door will be opened to you. 8 For everyone who asks receives; he who seeks finds; and to him who knocks, the door will be opened." Matthew 7:7–8*

Read: Matthew 9:1–8

I HOPE YOU HAVE SEEN BY NOW the connection between miracles and faith. Read Matthew 9:2 again closely. Whose faith moved Jesus to heal the man?....................................

....

If you said the men who carried the paralytic to Jesus, you are correct. It always inspires me when I read about their faith. They carried their friend to Jesus because they believed Jesus could heal him. This has huge implications for followers of Jesus. You may have friends who are not sure if God can heal them, but you can bring them to Jesus anyway. As you listen and care for those around you, you will hear stories of heartache and pain, some physical and otherwise.

After you care for your friends and if you listen thoroughly to them, you may want to ask, "Do you mind if I pray for you?" Most friends will say, "That would be fine." Sometimes people will say, "No, thanks." Don't be discouraged by that. But if they do agree, find a quiet place off to the side or in a parking lot or wherever it seems appropriate and bring their need to Jesus. Sometimes you will not pray for them at that time but later. The point is that you will want to ask God on their behalf to heal them. Your prayer can be something like this, "Heavenly Father, I bring [say his name] to you right now. He needs you to bring healing in [name the area] of his life. You spoke and the world came into existence. You have intervened many times and changed the course of history. I believe you can do it again. I ask You now to just say the word and heal [name]. We promise to give you all the honor and the glory for the healing. In Jesus' name we pray, amen." If you begin to ask God for healing, you will begin to see his supernatural intervention in your life and in the lives of those around you. It's pretty cool that God responds to our asking.

I want you to make another observation about this particular story. What did Jesus say after he saw their faith?..........
....

Does his response surprise you? I was expecting him to say, "Rise up and walk" but he says instead, "Take heart, son; your sins are forgiven." The rest of the story explains why Jesus did that. He wanted everyone to know that he can not only heal our bodies, he can also heal souls. He did say, "Get up, take your mat and go home." And the man did that and went home. The people praised God because of what Jesus did.

It is an awesome thing that Jesus is able to heal the whole person. God is changing your life, and he will change the lives of anyone who asks. Ultimately and in God's timing, we are all going to die a physical death. But if Jesus heals our souls by forgiving our sins, we will live forever with God. I love the verse in 1 John 1:9, "If we confess our sins, he is faithful and just and will forgive us our sins and purify us from all unrighteousness."

Why not take a few minutes right now to thank God for healing your soul by forgiving your sins. Take a few minutes also to begin praying for the needs of your friends. What a wonderful privilege it is to present your friends' needs to the one who holds the whole world in his hands. I won't write out a prayer for you this time. Just use your own words to communicate with God.

Attribute Three • Step Five
Give it Away

Scripture Memory:

7 " _____ _____ _____ _____ _____ _____ _____ ; _____ _____ _____ _____ _____ ;

_____ _____ _____ _____ _____ _____ _____ _____ . 8 _____ _____ _____

_____ _____ _____ ; _____ _____ _____ _____ ; _____ _____ _____ _____

_____ , _____ _____ _____ _____ . " _____ _____:_ - _

7 *"Ask and it will be given to you; seek and you will find; knock and the door will be opened to you.* 8 *For everyone who asks receives; he who seeks finds; and to him who knocks, the door will be opened." Matthew 7:7–8*

Read: Matthew 10:1–8

I HAVE OFTEN WONDERED HOW IT MUST HAVE FELT to be a follower of Jesus in person. It would have been amazing to see him perform miracles and to hear him speak. When you read this passage you see his intent that his followers would do as he did: preach the nearness of God's kingdom and perform miracles (healing, cleansing, driving out demons, et cetera). How would you have felt if Jesus said to you, "I give you authority to drive out evil spirits and to heal every disease and sickness"?...

....

I would have felt inadequate, excited, humbled, and hopeful at the same time. The most encouraging words to me are found in Matthew 10:8, "Freely you have received, freely give." Jesus expects us to give away what he has given to us. Gifts that we receive are to be used, not hoarded.

There are plenty of examples in the New Testament of how the disciples did heal people with the power of the Holy Spirit. One example is found in Acts 3. Read Acts 3:1–10. What stands out to you about this story?..........................

....

Praying for people to be healed is only giving away what God gives you. About two years into planting Elevation Church in Layton, Utah, my friend Jimmy came up to me before one of the Sunday morning gatherings at the movie theater. Jimmy asked me to pray for him as he had torn his shoulder all to shreds inside and was having surgery that week. I told him that we should not just pray for the surgery, but pray that God would just heal his shoulder so that he didn't need his surgery. We prayed at the bottom of the stadium seating in the theater soon after the service began. Jimmy came to me the next week and said he was really upset with me. I asked, "Why?" He said that God did heal his shoulder completely, so much so that the surgeon had opened him up, found nothing wrong and the doctors argued about the x-rays and MRIs before the surgery. They were going to still charge him for cutting into him. Jimmy said that the next time I had a harebrained idea to ask God to heal him, I should do it a lot sooner. I am telling you this not so you can be wowed at this gift, but so you will begin to ask God to heal you and others. Ask.

Read 1 Corinthians 12:4–11. It is really important to remember that God is always the hero. He just lets us be a part of the miracle. Reread 1 Corinthians 12:6. Who is it who works gifts in all men?

That's right! It's God and not us. We are just instruments through whom God works. It amazes me that God includes us in his work. He could just do it on his own but he lets us be part of it. That amazes me! I also want you to notice 1 Corinthians 12:9. Notice that "gifts" is plural. In other words, there is more than one gift of healing. God can do anything he wants through any of us. If the Spirit of God is in you, then the same God who spoke the world into existence can do great things through you. He is the same God. I have observed, however, that God tends to use some people more in one area of healing and other people in other areas. For example, I have prayed for people and have seen various types of healings, but I have a friend who God has more often used when he prayed for infertile couples to have children. I do not understand it, but it seems to be the case.

I need to address one last thing before we move on: the question, "Why does God heal one thing and not another?" Whole books are written on this subject.[1] I already mentioned that God healed me from a car accident and my allergies, but I also mentioned that God did not heal my knee. I had a painful sports injury where I tore a ligament, I prayed many times but God did not heal it. I also struggle with depression. It seems to be a genetic thing. I have prayed for healing in this area, but have not been healed yet. There are some who say we are not healed because of lack of faith. There is certainly a link between lack of faith and lack of healing. Matthew 13:58 describes what happened when Jesus went to his hometown, "And he did not do many miracles there because of their lack of faith." We need to be careful not to judge, however, because sometimes people have faith but God chooses not to heal. When this happens, one thing is certain. God's character never changes. Ten times in the Bible God is described as a "compassionate and gracious God, slow to anger and abounding in love" (Exodus 34:6; 2 Chronicles 30:9; Nehemiah 9:17; Psalms 86:15, 103:8, 111:4, 112:4, 145:8; Joel 2:13; Jonah 4:2). In other words, God's choice to heal one and not another is not based on his love and compassion for an individual. God is always loving and he always cares for you. When he chooses not to heal, I have two recommendations. First, trust him. Don't freak out and turn your back on him in anger. He is your best friend. Even if you turn your back on him, he will never turn his back on you. He loves you and you can trust him. Second, look for the good in the situation. You may not see it right away, perhaps never, but look for it anyway. I have clung to the truth of Romans 8:28 when life doesn't make sense: "And we know that in all things God works for the good of those who love him, who have been called according to his purpose." It doesn't say that "all things are good." It says that "in all things God works for the good of those who love him." So, ask God for healing; believe that he can heal; experience healing, and trust him when he chooses to not heal. This was a longer section today, but I want to pray for you.

Prayer:

Heavenly Father, thank you for your kindness in our lives. I am encouraged today, even while I am writing this, that your character never changes, that you are a gracious and compassionate God, slow to anger and abounding in love. We have been through a lot together, and you have always been kind to me. Even when you have allowed me to go through painful things, both physically and emotionally, you have been there for me. Help my friends who are reading this book to learn that about you as well. Help them to cling to you in times of joy and sorrow, when you heal and when you choose to do things differently from what we ask. Teach my friends to rejoice in you at all times and to find your corresponding peace because of it (Philippians 4:4–7). We need you at every turn in our lives. Give my friends faith to believe you are "able to do immeasurably more than all we ask or imagine, according to [your] power that is at work within us, to [you] be glory in the church and in Christ Jesus throughout all generations, for ever and ever! Amen" (Ephesians 3:20–21).

Attribute Three
Decisions

Attribute Four

•

Learn to Influence

Attribute Four • Introduction
Learn to Influence

THE CHURCH WHERE I BECAME A FOLLOWER OF JESUS believed your life should radically change when you start to follow Jesus. When Jesus Christ becomes your leader, he makes you a new person. The old has gone; the new has come. I believe that. I have seen this in people's lives, but never on the scale and magnitude of what I read about in the book of Acts.

As I read and reread the Gospels and Acts, three things stood out to me about influencing people for Christ. First, followers of Jesus are called to attract people to him. Jesus told his followers they are to be the salt of the earth and the light of the world (Matthew 5:13–16). Salt on food makes you want to come back for more. Light shows you the right path. Jesus embodied this. His teaching style was attractive. His personality was magnetic. The miracles he did and the way he cared for his disciples attracted people, causing them to want to follow him. He was "attractional."

Second, we need the empowerment of the Holy Spirit to be effective witnesses for Christ. After Jesus resurrected from the dead and before he ascended into heaven, Jesus told his disciples to wait until they had been empowered by the Holy Spirit (Acts 1:8). Jesus had given his followers an impossible task, "Make disciples of all nations" (Matthew 28:18–20). Think about it for a minute. There were no planes, trains, automobiles, mass mailing systems, televisions, telephones, or Internet. All they had was a changed life and a promise that when the Holy Spirit came on them, they would have power to witness effectively. At a large Jewish celebration called Pentecost just fifty days after Jesus' resurrection, it happened. The early followers of Jesus were in prayer, waiting for the empowerment of the Holy Spirit, when a supernatural wind filled the place where they were sitting. People saw something that looked like tongues of fire that separated and rested on everyone present. Every follower of Christ present began to speak in languages they had never learned.¹ People in the street heard what was happening and were surprised to hear someone in Jerusalem praising God in their native language when their native language was not the language spoken in Jerusalem. In the middle of that scene, Peter stood to address the growing crowd. Just fifty days prior, Peter denied being a follower of Jesus at nighttime to a servant girl. Yet in this story, he is able to stand before a crowd of thousands to challenge them to a decision to follow Jesus. That can happen when the Holy Spirit empowers a person. It can happen to you. About three thousand people made commitments to follow Christ that day and were baptized. That's an effective day.

Third, sharing Christ is personal. One exciting thing I discovered in my study was there are different styles for sharing your faith that are modeled in the New Testament: confrontational, intellectual, testimonial, relational, invitational, and serving. Your style of sharing Christ will look different from others. Each day we will explore a different style and then ask God to empower us by his Holy Spirit to share Christ effectively.

Take some time right now to ask God to empower you with the Holy Spirit like he did with the early followers of Jesus so you can be the most effective witness you can be. It is not something you should fear. Jesus said, "If you then, though you are evil, know how to give good gifts to your children, how much more will your Father in heaven give the

Holy Spirit to those who ask him!" (Luke 11:13).

Do not be surprised if the Holy Spirit enables you to do things you have never learned. It is not uncommon at all. In fact, it is normal and can be expected. If this whole thing is new to you or if you are uncomfortable about it, make it a matter of prayer. It should not produce anxiety in you. It is a good thing from God. He will lead you as you seek him. Feel free to talk with your spiritual coach if you have questions.

> ***Prayer:***
>
> Heavenly Father, I worship you today. There is none like you. You reached out to me, accepted me, forgave me, and you are changing my life. I ask you to empower me by your Holy Spirit today like you did your early followers. Completely baptize me in the Holy Spirit. Enable me to praise you beyond my own words and understanding. I want and need your power to be the witness you are calling me to be. There are people all around me who are hungry for you. Give me the ability to share Christ with them effectively. I wait for you now to empower me. (I encourage you to be responsive now to the work of the Holy Spirit in your life. If he gives you words to pray, pray them. If he gives you words that are beyond your understanding, say them. It is the Holy Spirit praying through you. When the Holy Spirit enables you to pray, it is a beautiful thing.)

Attribute Four • Step One
Invite People

Scripture Memory (new):

[18] Then Jesus came to them and said, "All authority in heaven and on earth has been given to me. [19] Therefore go and make disciples of all nations, baptizing them in the name of the Father and of the Son and of the Holy Spirit, [20] and teaching them to obey everything I have commanded you. And surely I am with you always, to the very end of the age." Matthew 28:18–20

Scripture Memory (review):   Matthew 4:19
            Matthew 11:28–30   Matthew 7:24–25
            Matthew 7:7–8

Take the Evangelism Styles Questionnaire on page 220.

Read: John 1:40–46

ONE OF THE MOST EXCITING THINGS you will ever do is bring a friend to Jesus. The excitement is not just yours. Jesus said, "There is rejoicing in the presence of the angels of God over one sinner who repents" (Luke 15:10). But how do you do that?

One of the most logical ways to bring people to Christ is to literally bring people to events where they can meet Christ, to church services, concerts, parties, et cetera. Studies show that people are most likely to follow Christ because of the influence of a friend or family member.[1] This is especially significant for parents with children, since 64 percent of people who follow Jesus said they made the decision before they were age 18.[2]

This is exactly what you see when Andrew met Jesus. John 1:41–42 reads, "The first thing Andrew did was to find his brother Simon and tell him, 'We have found the Messiah' (that is the Christ). And he brought him to Jesus." The Apostle Peter came to Jesus because his brother brought him.

Do you have some friends or family members you would like to introduce to Jesus?..

Is that something you would like to do?.........................

Who would you like to invite first?..............................

What are some logical ways you can invite someone to meet Jesus?...

....

I hope you feel comfortable bringing your friends to your church as part of how you introduce your friends to Christ.[3] At our church, Elevation, we do everything we can to make our Sunday gatherings guest-friendly. We have greeters and a continental breakfast to make people feel welcome. We try to provide helpful written information to help people understand who we are, before and after they attend. We attempt to use normal language when we teach about the Bible. We also invite everyone to a dinner once a month to help them get to know others and the church better.

Do you feel free to invite your friends and family to your church? Why or why not?..

What could your church do to make the gathering a better place to bring your friends and family?.........................

....

There are some practical steps you can take to start bringing your friends to Christ. First, make a list of your friends and family members who could benefit from a relationship with Jesus. There are four logical categories of people who are close to you. Write down who comes to your mind that you might want to introduce to Jesus:

• Friends..

....

....

• Family Members..

....

....

• Co-workers...

....

....

• Neighbors...

....

....

Second, continue to pray for them. Jesus said in John 6:44, "No one can come to me unless the Father who sent me draws him." No one loses their free will to accept or reject Christ, but you can pray for each person in the following ways:

→ Present the person to God by name as someone for whom he died.

→ Ask God to pull this person to himself, to open her eyes to the emptiness of life without him.

→ Ask God to help her see her need for forgiveness and to remove any confusion about God and the good life he offers.

→ Ask God to help her understand the meaning and the importance of Christ's finished work on the cross.

→ Ask God to open her heart to his love and truth.

You can also pray for yourself in the following ways:

→ Ask God to help you live a consistent and attractive Christian life.

→ Ask God to help you be authentic and honest as you deal with life's ups and downs.

→ Ask God to give you wisdom to know how to approach the relationship.

→ Ask God to grant you appropriate boldness and courage to communicate his love effectively.

→ Ask God to expand your knowledge so you will be ready to define and communicate God's message clearly.

→ Ask God to use you to lead this person into a relationship with Christ.

Prayer:
(Take a few minutes right now to pray for the people on your list using the suggestions above to guide you.)

Attribute Four • Step Two
Share Your Story

Scripture Memory:

¹⁸ Then _____ came to them and ____, "All authority in _____ and on earth __ __ _____ to me. ¹⁹ _____ go and ____ disciples of all nations, baptizing _____ in the name of the_____ and of the ____ and of the Holy _____, ²⁰ and teaching them to _____ everything I have commanded you. And _____ I am with you always, to the ____ end of the age." _____ 28:18–20

¹⁸ Then Jesus came to them and said, "All authority in heaven and on earth has been given to me. ¹⁹ Therefore go and make disciples of all nations, baptizing them in the name of the Father and of the Son and of the Holy Spirit, ²⁰ and teaching them to obey everything I have commanded you. And surely I am with you always, to the very end of the age."
Matthew 28:18–20

Read: John 9:1–25

E VERYONE'S STORY WITH JESUS IS DIFFERENT. As you look back on your life, you will probably see how God has been reaching out to you through circumstances, people, and experiences. Perhaps a friend or co-worker lived a different lifestyle that stood out to you and attracted you to Christ. Perhaps a friend or a family member showed you kindness or support during an important season in your life. While we all have the same need for forgiveness and relationship with God through Jesus, how someone becomes a follower of Christ is always unique.

There are at least four reasons why it is important for you to tell your story. First, it helps people around you know why your life is changing. Second, it brings honor to God. Although you are an important person in your story, God is really the hero. Only God can change a life. Third, it gives people hope that God can change their lives as well. Fourth, it is difficult for anyone to argue with your experience. While you may not have all the answers to their questions, you can share what you know, how Jesus is changing your life.

Based on John 9:1–2, what do you think the man's life was like before he met Jesus?..
....

How did Jesus change his life?..
....

The people who were questioning this man were well educated and powerful. Why was his story so powerful to them even though he was neither educated nor powerful?
....
....

Read John 9:35–38. How did this man become a believer in Jesus?..
....

What happened after the man believed?......................................
....
....

Take a few minutes now and write out your story using the following questions to guide you.

Writing Your Story

• Where were you spiritually before receiving Christ?

- How did that affect you—your feelings, attitudes, actions, and relationships?

- What caused you to begin considering Christ as a solution to your needs?

- What realization did you come to that finally motivated you to receive Christ?

- What did you do specifically to receive Christ?

- How has your life begun to change since you trusted Christ?

- What other benefits have you experienced since becoming a follower of Christ?

- Is there a passage of Scripture that means a lot to you now that you are a follower of Christ?

I have a few suggestions. First, share your story with your spiritual coach. It will be good practice even though you may have already told him or her. Second, take the time to write out your story in its entirety. I invite you to type it up and send it to me at this e-mail address: stories@elevation.cc. We really enjoy hearing how God changes people's lives. Let me know if you are comfortable with us sharing it with others. We may post it on a blog so people can hear how God is changing lives. Third, practice telling your story in private. Say it again and again until you are comfortable sharing it. Fourth, reduce your story. Most people will listen for about three minutes without feeling imposed upon. Less is best. Fifth, ask a friend or family member if you can share your story with him. When you are done, thank him for listening. Ask him what he thinks of your story. Tell him that if he ever wants to share his spiritual journey, you would enjoy hearing it.

Prayer:
Thank you, Heavenly Father, for changing my life. I know you are going to continue to change me as well. I lift my friends and family up to you right now. (Present them by name to God now.) Draw them to yourself. Use circumstances and situations to help them realize you love them and have a purpose for their lives. Help me to be an accurate witness of how you can change a life. I know I cannot do that on my own. Use me to bring people to you. Amen.

Attribute Four • Step Three
Be a Genuine Friend

Scripture Memory:

¹⁸ Then _____ came to ____ and ____, "All _____ in _____ and on ____ has ____ given to me. ¹⁹ _____ go and _____ _____ of all _____, baptizing _____ in the _____ of the _____ and of the ____ and of the _____ _____, ²⁰ and teaching _____ to _____ everything I have _____ you. And ____ I am ____ you _____, to the ____ end of the ____." Matthew ___:18–20

¹⁸ *Then Jesus came to them and said, "All authority in heaven and on earth has been given to me. ¹⁹ Therefore go and make disciples of all nations, baptizing them in the name of the Father and of the Son and of the Holy Spirit, ²⁰ and teaching them to obey everything I have commanded you. And surely I am with you always, to the very end of the age."*
Matthew 28:18–20

Read: Luke 5:27–30

THE PROBLEM I SEE WITH MOST CHRISTIANS is that they have separated themselves so much from the rest of the world that they do not know how to relate to the world. Following Jesus does lead us in a different path than the rest of the world, but as I read the New Testament I see that we are called to be *in* the world, not products of it. I am encouraged by what I saw in Jesus as I read. He was comfortable interacting with people from a variety of backgrounds and life situations. His primary mode was to love and accept people. He did not lower his standards. He was with people where they were and they were attracted to his life. As you allow Christ to do this through you, you will begin to see your friends come to Christ. People are much more open to Christ than you and I realize. Many people know something is missing in their lives but they don't know what it is. Unfortunately, many followers of Jesus stay away from people with other lifestyles than theirs. As a result, they are unable to have the impact Jesus said we should have. It is tough to tell people about Jesus if you are not their friend.

I want you to think for a minute about your best friend. What is he or she like? (If you don't have a best friend, think for a minute about the characteristics you would like to have in a friend.) ....

....

....

The book of Proverbs describes a good friend as one who has the following characteristics:

- Faithful and consistent (Proverbs 17:17)
- Keeps secrets (Proverbs 11:13, 25:9–10)
- Available and dependable (Proverbs 27:10, 18:24, 20:6, 25:19)
- Has gracious speech (Proverbs 22:11)
- Not easily annoyed but patient (Proverbs 12:16)
- One who understands you (Proverbs 20:5)
- One who helps you become a wiser person (Proverbs 27:17, 13:20)
- Generous (Proverbs 19:6, 11:25, 18:16, 19:6, 22:9)
- Sensitive to your feelings (Proverbs 25:20)

- A friend with your parents (Proverbs 27:10)
- Able to accept advice and a rebuke (Proverbs 13:10, 27:6)
- Pleasant to be around (Proverbs 27:9)

I don't know anyone who doesn't want a friend with the characteristics mentioned above. Which of these characteristics does your best friend have?..

....

....

Which characteristics would you like to see more of in your life?..

....

....

What kind of a friend was Levi according to Luke 5?

....

What does it tell you about Jesus that Levi was comfortable inviting Jesus to a banquet with his "sinner" friends?...

....

What do you think it meant that Jesus was a friend of sinners? (Luke 7:34)...

....

Are you a friend of sinners? How so?.....................................

....

Friendship is often enjoying something with another person. What are some things you like to do for fun that you could do with someone who hasn't yet made a commitment to Christ?..

....

Do you know anyone with whom you can enjoy that fun thing who needs Jesus?...

A good friend listens to you. Unfortunately, most of us are not good listeners. We all like to talk about ourselves and our ideas. However, as you are allowing Christ to change you, he is going to show you how to become more others-centered rather than self-centered. You will start to care more about the other person's story rather than the story you want to tell. I encourage you to practice listening to others by doing the following:

✧ When someone starts sharing something with you, stop and focus on her. Maintain comfortable eye contact. Face the person if it is appropriate. Let her know by your actions that what she is talking about is important to you.

✧ Summarize her content and feelings. You may use a phrase like, "Let me see if I understand you. Am I correct in saying…" Or, "It sounds like you were stressed at work today." If she says, "Well, that's really not it," then you didn't hear her correctly. Try again.

✧ Discipline yourself to focus on the person and her story rather than thinking about what you are going to say and a story you want to tell.

✧ Don't interrupt or complete the person's sentences.

✧ Don't be afraid of a few seconds of silence. Sometimes people need to think before they start talking again. Be patient.

✧ Don't be quick to give advice. Listen and care about the person. People are turned off by pushy and arrogant people. Giving a quick answer can feel like both.

Many people are open to Christ when they go through a crisis of some sort. If you have been a good friend before the crisis, your friend will trust you in a crisis. Offer to pray for your friend and be open to sharing Christ especially at that time.

Prayer:
Take a few minutes to ask God to help you be a better friend. Tell God aspects of friendship with which you need him to help you. Ask God to show you with whom you can spend time as a friend.

Attribute Four • Step Four
Speak Directly

Scripture Memory:

¹⁸ Then _____ came to ___ and ___, "All _____ in
_____ and on ___ ___ ___ ___ to me. ¹⁹ _____
go and _____ _____ of all _____, baptizing ____ in
the _____ of the _____ and of the ____ and of the ____
_____, ²⁰ and teaching _____ to _____ everything I have
_____ you. And _____ I am _____ you _____, to the
___ end of the ___." Matthew 28:___ – ___

---

*¹⁸ Then Jesus came to them and said, "All authority in heaven
and on earth has been given to me. ¹⁹ Therefore go and make
disciples of all nations, baptizing them in the name of the Father
and of the Son and of the Holy Spirit, ²⁰ and teaching them to
obey everything I have commanded you. And surely I am with
you always, to the very end of the age."*
Matthew 28:18–20

Read: Acts 2:1–41; 8:4–8, 26–40

WHAT COMES TO YOUR MIND when you think of the word
"evangelist"? Some of us think of televangelists or street
preachers. Millions of people in the United States and around
the world have decided to follow Christ because of the gifted
ministry of Billy Graham and others who speak directly about
the love of God. This is somewhat similar to what Peter did on

the day of Pentecost. Do not think, however, that the direct approach to sharing Christ has to be done by a trained professional in a stadium. It can be an individual speaking directly about Christ to a person in private like Phillip did with the Ethiopian eunuch. The direct approach works for some because they have not yet accepted Christ and are ready to respond. They just need an opportunity.

Every follower of Christ needs to learn how to share the message of Christ directly. While the direct approach may not be your primary mode, you need to be prepared to help people find Christ if they are ready.

The Gospel message is simple. Look up each passage of Scripture below and memorize the message. You may want to make a copy of it and put it in your Bible.

+ God loves you and has a wonderful plan for your life (1 John 4:16).

+ God is holy (1 Peter 1:16) and just (2 Thessalonians 1:6).

+ We were created holy but we became sinful (Romans 3:23).

+ Because of our sin, we deserve death (Romans 6:23).

+ It is only by God's gift of grace that we are able to be saved (Ephesians 2:8–9).

+ Jesus who was fully God became a man (John 1:1, 14), died in our place (1 Peter 3:18; 2 Corinthians 5:21), and offers forgiveness as a gift (Romans 6:23).

+ You must respond (John 1:12) by asking Christ to be your leader and forgiver (1 John 1:9, 1 Peter 3:15).

+ When you do that, the Holy Spirit will transform your life (2 Corinthians 5:17; 1 Corinthians 6:19-20).

Prayer:

Heavenly Father, I pray for boldness to share the message of Christ with people who do not yet know you. You have been good to me, and I want others to know about you. Help me to be aware of people around me who are open to Christ. Give me the courage to share with them. Give me an opportunity today to talk with someone about who you are and the difference you can make in our lives. Amen.

Attribute Four • Step Five
Serve People

Scripture Memory:

---

[18] *Then Jesus came to them and said, "All authority in heaven and on earth has been given to me.* [19] *Therefore go and make disciples of all nations, baptizing them in the name of the Father and of the Son and of the Holy Spirit,* [20] *and teaching them to obey everything I have commanded you. And surely I am with you always, to the very end of the age."*
Matthew 28:18–20

Read: John 13:1–17, 34–35; Acts 9

I HAVE SOME OF THE BEST FRIENDS a man could ever be blessed to have stand with him. When I had to move to Missouri, my friend Brian Yocum drove across the country in a van with no air conditioning to haul my stuff to my new place. When Ami (my wife) was pregnant and we needed help with putting sod on our yard, guess who showed up to help? Brian Yocum. When we needed to paint our nursery for the new baby, Brian showed up with his wife to help paint. When Brian comes over to visit and we are outside, he usually starts pulling any weeds that are in my flower beds. Every time Brian helps, we have tons of fun and it always feels like a huge gift. The impact Brian has had on my life is enormous. Because of his service, I want to help everyone around me, too. Being served can have that affect on people.

That's exactly what Jesus did for his disciples and the people around them. When he saw someone in need he served them. The key theme of the Gospel of Mark summarizes this aspect about Jesus: "For even the Son of Man did not come to be served, but to serve, and to give his life as a ransom for many" (Mark 10:45). One of the marks of followers of Christ is their service to others.

One of the most moving stories in the Bible that illustrates this aspect of Jesus is found in John 13:1–17. The disciples and Jesus arrived in Jerusalem for the Passover, a massive Jewish celebration that reminded the Jews how God miraculously brought them out of slavery in Egypt. Jesus and the disciples either borrowed or rented a room where they could have their Passover meal. Normally a servant would be present to wash people's feet as they came into the house, but none was present that day. Jesus surprised everyone by taking on the role of a servant and washing all the disciples' feet. Think about it for a minute. The Son of God, the one who spoke the world into existence, the one who would save the world, got down on his knees and washed the dirty feet of his disciples. By doing this, he demonstrated that no act of service was too low for him or us. John records Jesus teaching his disciples about this in John 13:14–17:

> Now that I, your Lord and Teacher, have washed your feet, you also should wash one another's feet. I have set you an example that you should do as I have done for you. I tell you the truth, no servant is greater than his master, nor is a messenger greater

than the one who sent him. Now that you know these things, you will be blessed if you do them.

What kinds of things come to your mind when you think about the call to serve people?......................................
....

Who around you needs to be served right now? What are their needs?...
....

Do you have any ideas about how you or others could serve others?...
....

What part of serving will be a challenge for you?............
....
....

Talk with your spiritual coach about how to get involved at your church. You could also serve your neighbors. What do they need help with? You could serve your family. What are their needs? What do you have to give?

When you serve, you are going to feel God's joy because that's how he designed us. Will you make a decision today to make your life about serving others?

Make that decision now before the Lord.

Prayer:

Jesus, it humbles me that you came to serve people. You are the Creator of the universe. You hold everything in your hand. You have all power and authority and yet you stoop down to wash feet, my dirty feet and my dirty heart. You came to this earth to forgive me of my sin, to show me how to have an abundant life, and to show me how I could be with you forever. Your serving me in those ways humbles me. It brings focus to my life, why I am here. It's not naturally in me to make my life about others. Even when I am serving others, it is often about me, wanting people to affirm me or thank me or appreciate me. I really need your help to learn how to serve in a way that is about you and the people I am serving. Teach me how to do that. Grow a servant's heart in me. Have your way in and through my life. Amen.

Attribute Four • Step Six
Make Sense

[18] *Then Jesus came to them and said, "All authority in heaven and on earth has been given to me.* [19] *Therefore go and make disciples of all nations, baptizing them in the name of the Father and of the Son and of the Holy Spirit,* [20] *and teaching them to obey everything I have commanded you. And surely I am with you always, to the very end of the age."*
Matthew 28:18–20

Read: Acts 17:16–34

THE YEAR BEFORE I GOT MARRIED I had two different encounters with family members that were completely opposite of each other. Both of these conversations involved me telling my relatives about my beliefs in Jesus and the Bible. They both even wanted me to prove my points and reasonings. This was exciting to me because I am a very logical person with almost everything I come across. One of my relatives wanted me to disprove her point of view based on what I believed. We had a very loving conversation and at the end, my relative said that she didn't believe what I believed because that was not what her church taught, and her church had done so much good that although she agreed with my reasoning she couldn't leave her church's beliefs. She told me that a good feeling inside you would lead you to truth, not reasoning. My other relative wanted to read more about what I said and eventually decided to follow Jesus after listening to all the facts and checking them out.

It was refreshing to me to discover that *reasoning* was not wrong. Acts 17:16–34 describes the Apostle Paul reasoning in the synagogue with the Jews and God-fearing Greeks and in the marketplace with the philosophers. The Bible never asks you to shut off your brain. Unfortunately, some are still propagating the lie that you cannot ask hard questions and be a follower of Christ.

How did the Apostle Paul reason with the people from Athens?...
....

What was the result of Paul's reasoning with the philosophers at the Areopagus?...
....

Don't miss Acts 17:34, "A few men became followers of Paul and believed. Among them was Dionysius, a member of the Areopagus, also a woman named Damaris, and a number of others."

Paul's reasoning enabled some to come to faith. Here is what you need to know if you happen to encounter a person who has lots of questions like me:

+ Love the person. Don't reject him and attack him because he has questions. Love and acceptance are more powerful than an argument.

✣ Acknowledge good questions.

✣ Do not be offended that someone asks a question about a sacred issue. It is not wrong to ask questions about God.

✣ You do not need to have all the answers. It is much better to say you do not know than to make up an answer. Detailed people notice small inconsistencies, and they enjoy pointing them out.

✣ Tell the person, "I don't know the answer to that question" when you do not have an answer. Tell him you will try to find an answer for his question and then do it. It is loving to try to help someone find an answer to his question. While there may not be a definitive answer for every tough question, there are usually plausible ones. Some of the authors who wrestle with hard questions are: Lee Strobel, Josh McDowell, C. S. Lewis, and Ravi Zacharias. You could also ask your spiritual coach or your pastor for help as well.

✣ You do not need to have a faith crisis because someone else has a difficult question. Stay close to Jesus. Let others' questions be their questions and yours be yours.

✣ Pray for your friend. God can move a person from non-believing to believing. He often uses circumstances that have nothing to do with an argument to help a person get unstuck.

Do not shy away from those with difficult questions and do not be threatened by them. They are probably seeking real answers, and they certainly need the friendship that the body of Christ offers. Pray specifically for your friends. Ask God for wisdom to know how to love each one of them, especially those who need God to make sense. It might take awhile but if you love them and include them, some will come to Christ.

Prayer:
Praise God for forgiving you and for welcoming you into his family. Tell the Lord about your friends who need him. Ask God how you can serve them and love them.

Attribute Four
Decisions

....
....
....
....
....
....
....
....
....
....
....
....
....
....
....
....
....
....
....
....
....
....
....
....
....
....
....
....
....
....
....

Attribute Five

•

Learn to Love

Attribute Five • Introduction
Learn to Love

D O YOU HAVE A FRIEND who HAS THAT WONDERFUL quality that the more you know them, the more you like them? You might not have recognized it at first, but the longer you hang out with the person, the more you appreciate them. Jesus is like that. The more you get to know him, the more you will love him, appreciate him, and want to be like him. That's partly why we spent two lessons encouraging you to get to know him. The foundation of everything else we are going to learn together flows out of your relationship with him. In one sense you never grow beyond that. It is always about remaining in him and enjoying your loving relationship with Jesus.

Because of what he gives to you, you realize you want to be able to give to him more of yourself out of gratitude. And, frankly, since life is so much better doing it his way, you don't want to hold anything back from him.

In the Overview of this book, where Attribute Two– Learn to Listen is summarized, we saw how being with Jesus leads us to people who need healing. Jesus healed and continues to heal people not only of spiritual pain but also of physical and emotional pain as well.

My wife grew up in a good family that was very loving to each other. When she was a senior in high school, she attended a church service where they talked about God's love for us. Her whole life she had seen God as someone who she had to work to please, but for the first time she heard about how much God loved her regardless of what she did or didn't do. This foreign concept gripped her heart and changed the way she looked at God.

Many times we try to gain God's love and acceptance by what we do or don't do. We work hard and harder but we will never feel like we actually earn it. My wife and I both have discovered that you cannot do anything to make God love you more or love you less. This kind of discovery will change your life. This idea that you and I have to work for God's love is a lie. You can be a follower of Jesus and still believe things that are not true. If you act on those lies, it will mess you up. The powerful truth is that because of Jesus' life, death, and resurrection, you are deeply loved, completely forgiven, fully pleasing, totally accepted by God, and absolutely complete in Christ.[1] You are secure and significant in Christ. I want you to be able to learn this at the beginning of your walk with God so you can enjoy, know, and love God for the rest of your life.

Jesus said, "The thief comes only to steal and kill and destroy; I have come that they may have life, and have it to the full" (John 10:10). The goal for this session is to help you understand the truth about who Jesus says you are so you can enjoy the full life he has planned for you. To do this, we need to do a little probing to see how deeply you believe certain common lies. You will take a brief self-scoring questionnaire each day to help you identify where you are with the lies. You will also discover the truth about those lies so you can walk in freedom from now on. Are you ready? I want to pray for you as you continue your journey.

Prayer:
Heavenly Father, I believe you are good. You have done so much for us in Jesus Christ. Help my friends

discover the truth about who you are and who they are in you so they can walk in freedom before you the rest of their life. Amen.

Attribute Five • Step One
Trust God

Scripture Memory (new):

[37] Jesus replied: "'Love the Lord your God with all your heart and with all your soul and with all your mind.' [38] This is the first and greatest commandment. [39] And the second is like it: 'Love your neighbor as yourself.'"
Matthew 22:37–39

Scripture Memory (review): Matthew 4:19
    Matthew 11:28–30   Matthew 7:24–25
    Matthew 7:7–8   Matthew 28:18–20

Take the Step 1–Trusting God Assessment on page 224.

Read: Luke 23:32–43

MANY PEOPLE STRUGGLE WITH BELIEVING God will forgive them. When we do not know we can be forgiven, there are only a few options for us. We might *work* to try to get God to like us and to forgive us (volunteer at church, help the poor, give money) in hopes that our good deeds will outweigh our bad deeds. We try to prove to God that we are worthy to be loved. But we always wonder if we did enough so we live under a cloud of fear. We might *ignore* the question of God's forgiveness, trying to not think about it. Since there is nothing we can do about it, why dwell on it? We might *minimize* our sin by saying "everyone does it" or "what I did wasn't as bad as..." We might get *angry at ourselves*. It is a terrible weight to remember what we have done. Some of us beat ourselves up emotionally or in other ways, thinking that if we hurt ourselves enough, maybe we will never do the bad deed again. We might even get *angry at God*. No one is perfect. "Since God is already upset with me for doing wrong, I might as well continue to do what pleases me." We might do even more things that we know displease God because we have given up trying to please him. We might *ask God to forgive* us as well.

What types of the responses do you see among the criminals crucified beside Jesus?...
....

What was Jesus' response to the criminal who asked Jesus to remember him?...
....

It is really important that you notice that Jesus accepted that criminal and that the criminal did nothing to deserve it. Jesus simply gave him the gift of forgiveness and relationship for eternity because he asked.

What is your normal response to dealing with memories of past failures?...
....

I have two different responses. I work harder or I give up. Fight or flight. I work hard to prove to God or others that I am worthy to be loved and if that doesn't get me anywhere, I just give up. In high school I studied hard and got good grades so that my achievements would show I was worthy to be honored. Sports followed in the same vein. I picked activities to work at only if I thought they would prove my worth; the feelings of happiness and self-worth were only temporary. I often thought, "There must be more to life than this." Have you ever felt that way? If so, what did you do to try to find meaning in life? ....

....

One of the problems with thinking this way is that we think our value is established by what we do rather than what Christ has done for us. When we do this, we live our lives based on a lie, that our worth is dependent on us and not God.

Read Romans 5:6–11

Jesus already paid the price for your sin. There is nothing you can do to make God love you more or love you less. No matter how hard you work or how perfectly or imperfectly you serve him, he will not love you any more or any less than he does right now. What are your initial reactions to that statement? ....

....

How will knowing this truth affect the way you respond to God ? ....

....

Prayer:
Thank you, Jesus, for dying on the cross for my sin. It amazes me that you would do that for me. Thank you for making me right before God and for giving me peace and your favor. I am truly grateful. Forgive me for trying to find my worth in something other than you. (You may want to confess some of these things right now if they come to your mind.) I choose to find my worth only in you from this day forward. I rest in you. Amen.

Attribute Five • Step Two
Seek God's Approval

Scripture Memory:

³⁷ Jesus replied: "'Love ____ ____ ____ ____ with all ____ heart and with ____ your soul and ____ all your ____.' ³⁸ This is the first and _____ commandment. ³⁹ And the second is ____ it: 'Love your _____ as yourself.'"
_____ 22:37–39

---

³⁷ Jesus replied: "'Love the Lord your God with all your heart and with all your soul and with all your mind.' ³⁸ This is the first and greatest commandment. ³⁹ And the second is like it: 'Love your neighbor as yourself.'"
Matthew 22:37–39

Take the Step 2–Seeking God Assessment on page 226.

Read: Matthew 9:9–13; Colossians 1:21–22

I AM A RECOVERING WANNA-BE ROCK STAR. I wanted to be liked and approved by so many people around me that my life was all about doing what would get me praise and attention. It was a terrible world to live in, not being able to say "no" to my involvement with groups and organizations because I wanted their approval.

My parents divorced when I was only four years old. They both remarried and started new families. This left me lost in the middle, so it felt, at least. I craved my parents' attention so badly that I would push myself to do things that they would praise me for. It was a crazy cycle I lived in: working for their attention and praise. The feeling never lasted long, so I would have to work harder at something else to get their attention and receive more praise.

These same feelings of wanting approval followed me into my relationship with others around me and with God. The more I felt looked up to or praised, the more I felt approved. The feeling didn't last long and so I had to keep working hard to receive more and more attention from the world around me. I felt that the only way God would approve of me is if I built great ministries, preached awesome sermons, had the best ideas for the church world, and understood my Bible better than others. I was working hard for something Jesus already gave me—his approval. He already approved of me. I just didn't know it.

You can see how Jesus thinks about people from the story you read today from Matthew 9:9–13. Matthew was a tax collector. To get that job, he had to collaborate with the hated Roman government so he could legally steal money from his friends and family. The tax amount was never published, so he could name his own price and pocket the excess after he gave the unpublished but required amount to Rome. People hated the tax collectors because they knew this was happening. But Jesus looked past all of that and he saw a person whom he loved. While Matthew was still in his sin, Jesus loved him and invited him to follow. Jesus also loved Matthew's friends who were equally in need. That's what Jesus is like. He has always been a friend of people like Matthew, his friends, and anyone else who knows they need forgiveness. He is a friend of sinners like me and you.

When you don't know that, it can really mess you up. If you want God's approval, you may try to work really hard. I was surprised and relieved to discover this way of thinking was directly related to a false belief: "I must be approved by certain others to feel good about myself."

According to Colossians 1:22, what has Jesus done for us? ....
....

The word "reconcile" means "to make friendly again, to settle a quarrel." Notice that "reconciled" is a past tense verb. According to this passage, what event reconciled you to God and what was the result? ....
....

It would be hard to describe how freeing it has been to discover that I do not have to work anymore to please God. Many people, Christians included, feel unloved, unaccepted, and lonely because they believe the lie that God's love and approval has to do with their behavior. Just so I make sure you get it, whose behavior makes you approved by God?

You can start your walk with Jesus by knowing the truth that God loves and approves of you because of what Jesus did for you. Because of what Jesus did for you, you are holy, without blemish, and free from accusation. Take a deep breath right now and think about and enjoy God's approval.

Write the following sentence on an index card and repeat it throughout the day: "I am deeply loved, completely forgiven, fully pleasing, totally accepted by God."

How will knowing this truth affect your life? ....
....
....

Prayer:
Thank you, Heavenly Father, for accepting what Christ did for me on the cross. I am grateful for your acceptance and approval because of that. I turn away from trying to perform to find my value. Help me to accept myself the way you accept me. Help me to focus

only on resting in you and enjoying your approval. Help me to accept those around me the way you accept them, to encourage them to be the individuals you have made them to be. I rest in your approval today. Amen.

Attribute Five • Step Three
Enjoy God's Acceptance

Scripture Memory:

³⁷ _____ replied: "'Love _____ _____ _____ _____ with all _____ _____and with _____ _____ _____ and _____ _____your _____.' ³⁸ This is the _____ and _____ _____ . ³⁹ And the second is _____ it: 'Love your _____ as _____.'"
Matthew _____:37–39

---

³⁷ Jesus replied: "'Love the Lord your God with all your heart and with all your soul and with all your mind.' ³⁸ This is the first and greatest commandment. ³⁹ And the second is like it: 'Love your neighbor as yourself.'"
Matthew 22:37–39

Take the Step 3–Enjoying God's Acceptance Assessment on page 228.

Read: Luke 7:36–50

THE STORY IN LUKE 7:36–50 MOVES ME every time I read it. Although the woman was obviously a "sinner," Jesus received her act of love without embarrassment, and he gave her salvation and peace. He accepted her, something the Pharisee, at whose home they were eating, could not do. In this story, Jesus makes the point that those who have been forgiven much, love much.

I have met many people who believe those who fail are

unworthy of love and deserve to be punished. They might not say it that bluntly, but their belief shows up in a variety of actions. They feel justified in condemning others who fail, including themselves. They may call others or themselves names, "I am so stupid for…" or, "He's such a loser…" They might make jokes or cutting remarks about others' failures or they make self-deprecating statements about their own shortcomings. They might say harsh words (verbally abuse) or they physically abuse themselves or others. But the bottom line is that someone around them has to pay when failure occurs. The thought behind that belief is this, "Those who fail are unworthy of love and deserve to be punished."[1]

That is also why it is hard to deal with ourselves when we fail. None of us is without sin. The truth is that none of us really want justice. I have heard it said, "We want justice for others but grace for ourselves." Romans 3:23 states, "All have sinned and fall short of the glory of God." Some try to convince themselves they do not sin but 1 John 1:8 tells us, "If we claim to be without sin, we deceive ourselves and the truth is not in us." Romans 6:23 tells us the payment for that sin, "For the wages of sin is death." Since we all have sinned and we all deserve death, we all have a problem. If we get justice, we will be separated from God forever. If we don't get justice then God would be a liar. So we are stuck. Furthermore, Hebrews 9:22 states, "Without the shedding of blood there is no forgiveness." Someone has to die so we do not have to be separated from our Creator. 1 John 4:10 tells us how Jesus Christ provides the solution for our dilemma.

Summarize 1 John 4:10 in your own words.…………………

…………………………………………………………………………

…………………………………………………………………………

God sent his Son Jesus to atone for our sins. "Atone" means "to make amends." God sent Jesus to make amends for our sins so we don't receive what we deserve—death and separation from God. It is sobering but it's awesome! God loves you and wants you to have a relationship with him so much that he even paid the price for everything you have done that was wrong: past, present, and future.

That sets up a new life paradigm for us. According to 1 John 4:11, what impact will God's atonement have on your relationships?..

....

....

Based on this passage, how might God's love affect the way you look at yourself when you fail?...........................

....

How might it affect the way you treat others when they fail?..

....

....

Have you ever seen this modeled? If so, describe what that person was like..

....

What liberated me and helped me understand God's love and acceptance was this thought: If we could work for God's approval and acceptance, Christ didn't have to die. Nothing I do can ever surpass the sacrifice of Jesus.

You are loved by God beyond what you can ever imagine, forgiven of everything; he is very pleased with you, and you are accepted by God![2] Think about that statement for the next couple of minutes and let that seep into your spirit. These thoughts changed each and every day for me; I pray that they change your days for the rest of your life.

Prayer:
Thank you, Heavenly Father, for sending Jesus to pay for my sins completely. I am truly grateful that you have accepted me and that I am complete in Christ. Thank

you for welcoming me and inviting me to talk with you right now, freely and openly. That means so much to me. Teach me how to extend the same love and acceptance to others that you freely give to me. Amen.

Attribute Five • Step Four
Partner with God to Change You

Scripture Memory:

³⁷ Jesus_____: "'Love ___ ____ ___ ___ with_____
____and with ___ ____ ___ and _____ ___your _____.'
³⁸ ___ is the ___ and _____ _____. ³⁹ And the
_____ is ___it: ' ___ your _____ as _____.'"
Matthew 22:__ – __

*³⁷ Jesus replied: "'Love the Lord your God with all your heart
and with all your soul and with all your mind.'³⁸ This is the first
and greatest commandment. ³⁹ And the second is like it: 'Love
your neighbor as yourself.'"
Matthew 22:37–39*

*Take the Step 4–Partnering with God to Change You
Assessment on page 230.*

Read: John 7:53–8:11; Titus 3:3–7

HAVE YOU EVER THOUGHT, "I AM WHAT I AM. I cannot
change"? Or, "That's the way I've always been, and
that's the way I'll always be"? Have you ever turned down an
offer to do something you really wanted because you did not
want to embarrass yourself or others if you failed? If so, your
sense of who you are and your opinion of your past failures
are keeping you from enjoying the life God has for you. Both
of the passages you read today provide hope for you. With

God's help, you can change.

To move out of this kind of thinking and into the new life God has for you, you need a perspective that is based on God's unconditional love and acceptance. Your past failures are a reality, but so is God's unconditional love. To move out of feeling shameful about yourself, you will need to value God's view of you more than your view of your past failures.

You know you are struggling with this kind of thinking if you are not pursuing something you really want or need because you are afraid of rejection or failure. The threat of rejection may cause you to withdraw from people and social situations, especially if you are afraid you just won't measure up.

Those who struggle with this way of thinking often struggle with a sense of inferiority, habitually destructive behavior, self-pity, passivity, isolation and withdrawal, loss of creativity, codependent relationships, and despising their appearance.[1]

God has a much better way. It is called "regeneration." The moment you began to trust Christ, he made you a new person. 2 Corinthians 5:17 says, "Therefore, if anyone is in Christ, he is a new creation; the old has gone, the new has come!" Everything you and I have ever done was completely forgiven when we trusted Christ. Everything! Because you are no longer held captive by your past and because you are a new person in Christ, you can change. Say out loud, "Because I'm a new person in Christ, I can change. I no longer need to experience the pain of shame."

What did Jesus say to the woman caught in adultery after everyone left? ....
....

Notice that while others would condemn her to die, Jesus defended her right to live and then gave her hope that she could start a new life. Jesus does that for you as well.

Change may not be easy but it will be worth it. In order to change you need to internalize what God's Word says about you. Summarize Titus 3:3 in your own words.............

....

....

According to Titus 3:4–5, what prompted God to save you and how did he do it? ....

....

....

It is really important that you realize and accept that Jesus saved you not because of righteous things you have done but because of his mercy. Notice that "he saved us" is in the past tense. Jesus did the work to save all of us "by the washing of rebirth and renewal by the Holy Spirit." He washed you and renewed you. You may not always feel like a new person but God's Word tells you the truth about yourself. He gave renewal to you as a gift. That was God's part.

God's kindness makes you want to serve him. God gives you a gift (grace) and your response is gratitude. According to Romans 12:1–2, what is your part in the renewal process?...

....

What do these verses say is your response to God's mercy?...

....

What needs to happen so you no longer conform to the pattern of this world?...

....

What will happen when you do this?.............................

....

Why not talk to God right now about your decision to present your body to him. He sees your heart and he will help you change.

Prayer:

Dear Heavenly Father, I am amazed by your kindness and love for me. Thank you for saving me, not because of anything I did but because of your mercy. Thank you for washing my life and for renewing me by your Holy Spirit. I accept this as a gift from you. In view of your mercy, I present my body to you as a living sacrifice. Make me holy and pleasing to you. Renew my mind as well so I can think differently about my life. I want to change. Amen.

Attribute Five • Step Five
Enjoy God's Peace

Scripture Memory:

37 _____ _____ : " _____ _____ _____ _____ _____ _____ _____ _____ _____

_____ _____ _____ _____ _____ _____ _____ _____ _____ ,

38 _____ _____ _____ _____ _____ . 39 _____ _____

_____ _____ _____ : ' _____ _____ _____ _____ . ' "

_____ _____ : _____ – _____

---

37 Jesus replied: "'Love the Lord your God with all your heart and with all your soul and with all your mind.' 38 This is the first and greatest commandment. 39 And the second is like it: 'Love your neighbor as yourself.'"
Matthew 22:37–39

Read: Philippians 4:4–7

A s you study this attribute, you may be reframing what you believe about yourself and others by what God says about us. You have explored four lies that can keep you from the abundant life that God offers through Jesus. Today, you will learn how to be free from worry and anxiety. See if you can identify the four commands in Philippians 4:4–7.

....

....

This passage teaches us that God can help us learn how to be at peace in all circumstances. The four commands show us how: rejoice (v. 4), be gentle (v. 5), do not be anxious

(v. 6), present your requests to God (pray) (v. 6).

Let's be honest. We are not always happy. Painful and difficult things happen that make us sad, confused, or angry. What kinds of things are you going through right now that do not make you happy?..

....

It is critically important that you understand the difference between being happy and rejoicing in the Lord. Happiness is dependent on your circumstances. For example, I am happy when my daughters behave in public, but I am not happy when someone criticizes me. You can rejoice in the Lord, however, all the time because he is in control of life's situations. The truth of Romans 8:28 helps me with this, "And we know that in all things God works for the good of those who love him, who have been called according to his purpose." No matter what comes your way, happy or sad, you can always trust God to work things out for the good if you love him. The question you need to ask yourself is, "Do I love God?" If you love him, you can depend on him always. Faithfulness is part of God's character. Your joy is not dependent on your circumstances. It depends on God's character and that never changes. That's why you can rejoice in the Lord always.

Second, when someone hurts you, don't you sometimes want to hurt them back? This passage teaches us that you can always be gentle to everyone. The Greek word for "gentle" means "to show forbearance toward someone." It is the quality shown by friends who know one another's idiosyncrasies and weaknesses but like each other anyway. Harshness, on the other hand, can be expected from an enemy. Don't confuse gentleness, however, with weakness. You can be gentle and still do the tough thing. It takes real strength to treat others gently, even when they deserve otherwise. This passage says you can be gentle to everyone because the Lord is near. In what situations or with whom do you struggle being gentle? ....

....

Third, this passage teaches us that we do not ever have to be anxious. Anxiety is worrying about things you cannot change. Jesus taught his followers that worrying is worthless. It doesn't change a thing. He said, "Who of you by worrying can add a single hour to his life?" (Matthew 6:27). The assumed answer to that question of course is, "No one." Corrie Ten Boom, a Holocaust survivor said, "Worry does not empty tomorrow of its sorrow, it empties today of its strength." If you put your life in God's hands, you can trust him to take care of you. Change what you have the power to change and leave the rest with God.

What kinds of things are causing you anxiety right now? ....

....

....

Finally, the best way to handle anxious thoughts is to present them to God. That's another way of saying "pray." Talk to God about the things that are on your mind. You can tell him exactly what you are thinking and how you feel. I do a lot of this in my confidential journal. Whether you do it in writing or out loud, just pour out your soul to God. Tell him how you feel and what you are thinking. He already knows, but it is emotionally healthy to get it out. God can handle your struggles. He is strong.

The result of rejoicing, being gentle, not being anxious, and presenting your requests to God will be peace, "The peace of God, which transcends all understanding, will guard your hearts and your minds in Christ Jesus." God's peace will guard your mind. You can be joyful, gentle, and free from anxiety at all times and in all circumstances. Let the truth of that start to sink into your mind right now.

Prayer:
Take some time right now to talk with God about whatever is on your mind.

Attribute Five
Decisions

Attribute Six

•

Learn to Pray

Attribute Six • Introduction
Learn to Pray

GREAT FRIENDS ARE A SPECIAL GIFT. Friends are the ones you call first when the doctor gives you bad news or when you get a promotion. You can share your joys and sorrows with them without wondering if they will judge you or think less of you. They tell you when you have food on your face and when they think you are out of line. They also celebrate with you when you have a significant milestone. You might not see them for years, but when you get together, it is like you have never been apart. Great friendship is amazing.

I have that kind of friendship with one of my mentors, Doyle. Doyle is older than me by more than twenty years and he lives a state away, but we have a great friendship. He serves as a spiritual father to me in life, someone who understands my trials as church leader, and he's an encourager. He also can get in my face and let me know when I'm out of line. He is an amazing gift from God in my life. Our phone conversations and face-to-face times are good for my soul.

Doyle is constantly teaching me even when he isn't trying to teach me. Just living life with him helps me to soak in the life he has following Jesus. I thought you might enjoy reading part of an e-mail he sent me one fourth of July:

> Hey my friend, how was service or community or gathering or bunch of dudes and dudettes or what is it you call that time

together on Sunday mornings? There are great memories of when God jacked my reality during a prayer meeting that wasn't seeker-sensitive or post-modern or emergent, it was just a time when God met me and shook my world.

There was a time when I was just hungry for a change in my life, to see God take what was in me that wasn't of Him and remove it! It only came with a gut-wrenching time of prayer that wasn't scheduled or planned out with a strategy, just desperate for Him to show up and change me! I'm hungry for God to split my reality wide open again; to know Him as He intends.

I remember when I was in my late teens and going to church in my hometown. We would have Sunday evening service and then of course the altar call, but after the altar call we would have "afterglow" after that. It wasn't food after the service, it was staying around the altar in the afterglow of what God did during the service and altar. It was like bathing in the presence of God, just staying in the flow. Man, it was incredible.

The present times are uncertain, even scary without the peace of God. I know that I am my Father's son and that He gave His best so that I could have a complete life this side of heaven.

My buddy Doyle always leads me to want to know Jesus more. I don't know about you, but reading that makes me want to dive into prayer. Let's do that now.

Prayer:
Jesus, we join your followers who once asked you, "Lord, teach us to pray." We ask that you will teach us like you taught them. We want to draw close to you and to hear your thoughts. We also want our lives to align

with your plans for us. So teach us. Thank you for the invitation to follow you into a deeper walk with the Father. Amen.

Attribute Six • Step One
Decide Not to Pray Bad Prayers

Scripture Memory (new):

[9] "This, then, is how you should pray: 'Our Father in heaven, hallowed be your name, [10] your kingdom come, your will be done on earth as it is in heaven. [11] Give us today our daily bread. [12] Forgive us our debts, as we also have forgiven our debtors. [13] And lead us not into temptation, but deliver us from the evil one.'" Matthew 6:9–13

Scripture Memory (review):   Matthew 4:19
      Matthew 11:28–30   Matthew 7:24–25
      Matthew 7:7–8   Matthew 28:18–20
      Matthew 22:37–39

Read: Matthew 6:5–8

PRAYER IS SIMPLY TALKING WITH AND LISTENING TO GOD. Does it surprise you that Jesus teaches them how *not* to pray? In these verses, what does Jesus say not to do when you pray?

Jesus made it clear that prayer is not supposed to be something you do to display your spirituality. When you do that, prayer becomes about you. That is exactly what prayer is not. That's not to say you should never pray in public. It should just never be something you do to look holy. No one is holy except Jesus. When you talk with God in private, however, your Heavenly Father will reward you.

Jesus also taught in Matthew 6:7 not to "keep on babbling like pagans, for they think they will be heard because of their many words." Some people think they will get God's attention if they ask over and over, if they just bug him enough. Jesus was kind enough to tell us we cannot manipulate God to do anything just because we ask him a thousand times. God already knows our needs before we ask (Matthew 6:8).

I know I already talked about having a quiet time, but I want to keep it in front of you so it becomes a habit. Getting alone with God is something everyone can do. You may need to get up fifteen minutes earlier in the morning but you can do it. To pray like Jesus, you will need to find a time and a place that you will not be disturbed. I like to unwind at night by reading my Bible and praying. I love processing the events of the day through prayer with God. I find it helpful to get away from the television and the computer so I am not distracted. What time and place works best for you?.............

Prayer:
Take time right now to talk with God about your desire to continue to learn to pray.

Attribute Six • Step Two
Learn the Disciples' Prayer—Part 1

Scripture Memory:

⁹ "This, then, is how you should ____: 'Our _____ in heaven, _____ be your ____, ¹⁰ your _____ come, your ____ be done on _____ as it is in _____. ¹¹ Give us today our____ ____. ¹² Forgive us ___ debts, as we also have _____ our debtors. ¹³ And lead us not ____ _____, but _____ us from the evil one.'" _____ 6:9–13

---

⁹ *"This, then, is how you should pray: 'Our Father in heaven, hallowed be your name, ¹⁰ your kingdom come, your will be done on earth as it is in heaven. ¹¹ Give us today our daily bread. ¹² Forgive us our debts, as we also have forgiven our debtors. ¹³ And lead us not into temptation, but deliver us from the evil one.'"*
Matthew 6:9–13

Read: Matthew 6:9–13

WHEN YOU ARE LEARNING A NEW SKILL, excellent instruction is invaluable. That's why people will often take a skiing lesson before they hit the slopes for the first time. My oldest daughter Madison is a great skier for a little kid. I put her in private lessons at a ski resort in Park City when she was three years old. They taught her that wedging your skis to look like a pizza slice was how you stopped. Putting your skis side by side to look like two french fries was how you go down the mountain. After her lessons I went skiing down the bunny hill with her a few times. She would giggle the whole time and not listen to a thing I said, she just wanted to show me that she could ski. She was flying down the mountain one time and crashed hard. I skied up to her and told her that she was going to get really hurt skiing so fast. Her response was, "Dad, it's just snow." I found myself yelling "pizza" at the top of my lungs the whole time I would ski with her because she had no sense of fear on that ski slope. I was sore after skiing with her from all the falls I was taking trying to cut her off from heading for danger. I felt awkward trying to keep up with her, but all she needed was those lessons to give her confidence to ski.

Learning to pray is like learning to ski. You may feel awkward and uneasy, but a little instruction can go a long way.

In one sense, prayer is easy. It is simply talking to God about what's on your mind and then listening to whatever he says to you through his words (the Bible), through your thoughts, or through others.

The first followers of Jesus wanted to learn how to pray so they asked Jesus to teach them (Luke 11:1). We have already talked about the Lord's Prayer in the Overview of Attribute Six. In the next two days we are going to unpack that a little so you can learn how to pray with as little pain as possible. Jesus taught his followers six things about prayer. There are three Rs and three Fs. We'll talk about the three Rs today and the three Fs tomorrow.

Relationship—"Our Father in Heaven" teaches us that we are in a loving relationship with our Heavenly Father. Your Heavenly Father loves you so much. He longs for you to turn to him and to enjoy his presence. He welcomes you and enjoys being with you regardless of what you are going through, negative or positive. He cares about all your concerns. You may or may not have had a good father. But

God will never leave you or forsake you. I know I already mentioned God's compassion in Attribute Three–Step 5, but I never get tired of hearing it: "The LORD is compassionate and gracious; slow to anger, abounding in love." Any other view of God needs to be set aside in view of an accurate one.

Take a minute or two right now and thank God for being your Heavenly Father. Tell him that you love him and that you are grateful that he is caring for you. Open your heart to him.

Respect—"Hallowed be your name" teaches us that God is completely pure (holy) and as such is worthy to receive our honor and respect. Something good happens when we start with honoring and respecting God. Don't start with talking about your needs in prayer. We will get to that later, but it should not be the first thing. Tell the Lord how much he means to you and honor him. You may want to kneel right now to show your respect to God. Some people will sing a song or two to God. There are a variety of worship styles. I like songs like "He Reigns,"[1] "O Praise Him (All This For A King),"[2] "God of Wonders,"[3] "Indescribable."[4] (You can purchase these from iTunes for about one dollar each.) Pour out your love and respect as you sing to God. Don't hold back here. He is worthy of all the honor and glory you and I can give him and more. When you meet with your coach, ask them if they have some favorite songs or other ways they respect and honor God.

Take time right now to tell the Lord you honor him and respect him. Acknowledge that he is completely pure and that he never has a bad thought or a bad idea. Honor him with your whole heart.

Reign—"Let your kingdom come" teaches us to start with what God wants. You were not designed to "pull your own strings." When you pray "let your kingdom come," you are inviting God to be your leader and guide, to rule your life. You bow your life before him and you affirm that you belong to God, that you are committed to doing things his way. When you pray "let your kingdom come," you are inviting God to have complete control of your life.

Take time right now to ask God to rule in every area of your life. Talk with God about areas in your life over which you have difficulty giving up control: a job, a relationship, your future. You may find it helpful to write them down and then to share them with your coach.

Attribute Six • Step Three
Learn the Disciples' Prayer—Part 2

Scripture Memory:

⁹ "This, ____ , is ____ you should ____ : ' ___ _____ in
_____ , _____ be your _____ , ¹⁰ your _____ _____ ,
your ___ be ___ ___ _____ as it is in _____. ¹¹ ___ __
today our____ ____ .¹² _____ __ __ debts, as we also have
_____ our _____ . ¹³ ___ ___ __ __ _____ _____ ,
but _____ us ___ the ___ one.'" Matthew__:9–13

---

⁹ "This, then, is how you should pray: 'Our Father in heaven,
hallowed be your name, ¹⁰ your kingdom come, your will be done
on earth as it is in heaven. ¹¹ Give us today our daily bread. ¹²
Forgive us our debts, as we also have forgiven our debtors. ¹³ And
lead us not into temptation, but deliver us from the evil one.'"
Matthew 6:9–13

Read: Matthew 6:9–13

IN THE PREVIOUS STEP, WE TALKED ABOUT the three Rs of
prayer. Can you remember what they are?......................
....

Take a few minutes now and pray the three Rs: Relationship, Respect, and Reign. Review yesterday if you need to.

In this step, we are going to talk about the three Fs.

Food—"Give us today our daily bread" teaches us that
we can ask God to meet our basic needs. When our lives are
lined up with his values, we can ask for fuel to do it. You may

not be concerned today about whether or not you will have food. Most Americans have that covered pretty well...better than well. A group of friends of mine went to Fiji for a missions trip. When they got back one of them began to describe the living conditions of the natives. He said they lived in these little ten-by-ten foot houses with nothing in them but a rug to sleep on. He said that every morning they pray to God to provide their food, then they go out and pick the fruits, go fishing, and they have what they need for the day. They truly believe that God will provide for them for that day. Maybe our consumption of food should be a matter of prayer. What we have and what we don't. I am starting to see that eating is not about me, how I feel, how much I like or dislike something. It is about God providing me with the energy and strength to fulfill God's purpose for my life. (That will make you think about how much you spend on going out to eat.) When our hearts are aligned with God's heart, we can ask the Lord for food to help us. Take a moment right now and ask God to give you the food you need today to do his will for your life. How are you with food? Talk about this with your spiritual coach when you meet.

Forgiveness—"Forgive us our debts as we also have forgiven our debtors" teaches us that when we pray we remember we need forgiveness as much as everyone else. I often forget this. When people hurt those I love and care for, I tend to hold a grudge. The resentment I would hold in my heart was killing me emotionally and spiritually. Forgiveness is not forgetting, nor is it trusting someone. Forgiveness is choosing to not make a person pay for what they did. It is letting them off the hook—letting it go. It is not saying you should get back into a similar situation and allow them to hurt you or abuse you again. You may not trust someone because they are not trustworthy, but you can still forgive them. What helped me more than anything was realizing that I deserved punishment for all my sins. God in his mercy paid the price for all my sins, and yours as well, through the death of Jesus Christ on the cross. I do not deserve his forgiveness, but he gives it to me if I will receive it. Complete forgiveness is available to all through Jesus. You cannot pay for your sins. Jesus already paid for them. Because he did that for you, you can forgive others. Tremendous freedom awaits you. You don't have to hate anymore.

Freedom—"And lead us not into temptation but deliver us from the evil one" teaches us that God can help you win over every temptation. Most Americans think freedom means being able to do what you want whenever you want. This is not freedom. Proverbs 14:12 states, "There is a way that seems right to a man, but in the end it leads to death." In other words, if you do what you think is right, eventually it will lead to destruction. Real freedom is being able to please God with the way you live, the reason for which you were created. With God's help we can be delivered from the things that are destroying us. That's why we need to ask for freedom from temptation and deliverance from the evil one. We need God's help to go in the right direction and to do the right things. If you ask God, he will help you with this.

Let the Lord's Prayer guide you as you talk with God now.

Prayer:

(*Relationship*) Thank you, Heavenly Father, for inviting me to be your child. It is wonderful to know you welcome me and care for me.

(*Respect*) Truly you are pure and worthy of all praise and honor. There is no one like you. You are amazing. I worship you with my whole being.

(*Reign*) I invite you to rule in my life today. Have your way in me. Mold me and shape me in a way that brings honor to you. I invite you to have complete control of my life. Have your way in my home. Help me to love those around me like you want them to be loved.

(*Food*) Thank you for providing for my physical needs today, for food, shelter, and clothing. I have everything I need because you provide it. Help me to use every ounce of energy and all my resources for your purposes today.

(*Forgiveness*) Thank you for forgiving all my sins. (Admit to God any specific things you have done recently that you know are wrong.) I accept your complete forgiveness for my sins because of what Jesus did on the cross. Thank you. I forgive (name the person[s] you need to forgive) for (describe to God what the person did that hurt you). Because you forgive me, I can forgive them.

(*Freedom*) Guide me down the right path today. Help me to stay away from things that are destructive. Deliver me from (name the specific thing that you need freedom from). Thank you for the freedom I have because of the finished work of Jesus Christ. I am a new person today because of what you have done for me. I ask this in Jesus' name, amen.

Attribute Six • Step Four
Learn to Pray Through Pain

Scripture Memory:

⁹ "This, ____ , is ____ ____ ____ ____ : ' ____ ____ in ____ , ____ __ ____ ____ , ¹⁰ your ____ ____ ____ , your ____ be ____ ____ ____ as __ __ __ ____ . ¹¹ ____ __ ____ our ____ ____ . ¹² ____ __ __ ____ , as we also have ____ our ____ . ¹³ And ____ __ __ ____ ____ , but ____ us ____ the ____ one.'" Matthew 6:__–__

---

⁹ "*This, then, is how you should pray: 'Our Father in heaven, hallowed be your name, ¹⁰ your kingdom come, your will be done on earth as it is in heaven. ¹¹ Give us today our daily bread. ¹² Forgive us our debts, as we also have forgiven our debtors. ¹³ And lead us not into temptation, but deliver us from the evil one.'"*
Matthew 6:9–13

Read: Matthew 6:14–15

THERE WAS A TIME WHERE I WAS COMPLETELY sour in the forgiveness department. Someone whom had I looked up to in my life had deeply hurt me, but beyond that had hurt my family. I knew I needed to forgive. I tried to. I sat the person down at one point and apologized for all the things I had done wrong in the situations that had caused me and my family pain. He never apologized to me or tried to heal the past. It burned in me even more. I just didn't know how to forgive this person at all.

In the movie *The Karate Kid, Part II*, Mr. Miyagi has this great quote: "For man with no forgiveness in heart, life worse punishment than death." That was what was happening to me. This situation was eating me up inside. I prayed to God to show me how to forgive. It didn't happen overnight, but over time as I opened my heart up to God I realized that forgiveness wasn't about the other person. It was about me. Forgiveness was a gift to myself, not the other person. Forgiveness cut the strings this other person had over my life. It may take some time for you to work through the pain of your past. It may take you quite awhile to forgive everyone who has wronged you. It took me months, but I feel so much freedom from the actions of others. I really feel like a new person.

Write down the persons or incidents you know you need to forgive. Don't wait. Do it now. You will probably add to your list as you remember things later.............................

....

....

....

....

Take one incident at a time to pray through this process:

1. ***Pour out your soul to God*** (Psalms 13, 51:17). Tell God about the specific event that caused you pain. Pour it out. Tell him what happened and how you felt about it. Tell God about it until you know you have said everything that needs to be said. Don't censor yourself. God can take it. It might surprise you to find out there is a specific kind of psalm that is designed to help you pour out your heart to God when you are in pain. It is called a "lament" psalm. There are more laments than any other type of psalm.[1] This ought to encourage you to be open with God about your pain. Tell him or write out what you think about what happened to you. (I find writing is more helpful to me. I can look at it

and see it when I am done.) Tell God exactly how you feel. You can tell God your thoughts, pain, and concerns without worrying that he will be offended or shocked. It is healthy for you emotionally and spiritually to pour out your soul to God.

2. *Let God comfort you* (2 Corinthians 1:3–4). After you have poured out your heart, invite God into the painful memory. Ask God what he thinks about your painful situation. Listen to your thoughts and impressions at that point. He may remind you of a passage of Scripture. He may give you a new thought. He may give you a comforting picture. It is always different for me. Nothing can separate you from the love of God (Romans 8:39).

3. *Confess your sin* (1 John 1:9). What happened to you may have been sad or terrible, something that was not your fault. However, we all need to take responsibility for what we did afterwards. I hated people and tried to work harder to convince myself that I was worthy to be loved. That was against God's plan for my life. It was sin. You need to confess whatever you did as a result of your situation that was against God's principles. Confession is just agreeing with God that something you did was not right.

4. *Ask God to restore your soul* (Psalm 23:3; 2 Corinthians 5:17). 2 Corinthians 5:17 says, "Therefore, if anyone is in Christ, he is a new creation; the old has gone, the new has come!" Rest for a few minutes in God's presence, knowing that you are restored to relationship with God.

5. *Identify the lie* (2 Corinthians 10:4–5; John 8:32). Behind every sinful act is a lie, something you believe about yourself, God, or another that is not true. As you think about the painful incident, what are your thoughts? You may want to write them down. What you told yourself as a result of the painful incident may hurt more than the incident itself. If you can identify the lie, you can replace it with the truth.

You may need help from your spiritual coach, a pastor, or a counselor to identify the lie, but it is worth exposing it because the truth will set you free. I will give you an example. Growing up, I got teased a lot for my physical appearance. I was, and am still, very skinny and when I was a kid my head hadn't grown into my ears yet. A skinny kid with big ears, lots of freckles, and big feet. I believed the lies I heard growing up: that I was ugly and thus not worth loving. My family members didn't know I was getting made fun of at school and they would tease me at home as well, so the lie would gain more roots in my life. God helped me expose this as a lie. It would take too long to explore the ramifications of believing that lie, but I had to identify it so I could be set free by the truth.

6. *Replace the lie with truth* (Psalm 1; Philippians 4:4–9). You may need help to identify the truth about your situation. Talk this through with your spiritual coach. If he or she doesn't know, both of you can ask your small group leader or your pastor. If they can't figure it out, you may want to go to a good Christian counselor. There are several passages of Scripture that helped me replace my lie with the truth. Psalm 139:13–16 was powerful for me:

> For you created my inmost being; you knit me together in my mother's womb. I praise you because I am fearfully and wonderfully made; your works are wonderful, I know that full well. My frame was not hidden from you when I was made in the secret place. When I was woven together in the depths of the earth, your eyes saw my unformed body. All the days ordained for me were written in your book before one of them came to be.

According to God's Word, I was not a mistake. God thought about every day of my life before I was born. My physical appearance was even something that God had designed and made. The Master Craftsman had designed me! When I start to feel insecure, I can tell myself the truth. God loves me. He designed me. I'm here for a purpose. I am secure in him. That truth changed my life.

> **Prayer:**
> Do you have some people or situations that you need to pray through? Your caring Heavenly Father can set you free through the process you have learned today. He used it to change my life. It may take months for you to get through your list but when you are done you will feel like a new person. And you will never want to go back to the old way. When you come to Jesus, you find rest for your soul. Why not take one incident or a person on your list and walk through the process right now. Freedom awaits you.

Attribute Six • Step Five
Learn to Do Spiritual Warfare

Scripture Memory:

---

9 "This, then, is how you should pray: 'Our Father in heaven, hallowed be your name, 10 your kingdom come, your will be done on earth as it is in heaven. 11 Give us today our daily bread. 12 Forgive us our debts, as we also have forgiven our debtors. 13 And lead us not into temptation, but deliver us from the evil one.'" Matthew 6:9–13

Read: Ephesians 6:10–20

THE BIBLE TEACHES THERE IS MORE TO THIS WORLD than what you see. There is a real devil. There are rulers, authorities, and dark powers in this world and spiritual forces of evil in the heavenly realms (Ephesians 6:12). I wish it wasn't so but it is. Their sole purpose is to resist the work of God and to destroy your life. The evil one and his forces fight dirty. Rarely do they attack head on. When you are tired, hungry, or lonely, they move in to try to mess up your life. Ephesians 6:10–20 shows you how to fight and win against these destructive forces. There are eight commands in this passage that show you how to win.

Read Ephesians 6:10 again. What are we commanded to do?..

....

It is absolutely essential to know from where your strength comes. Notice it does not come from within you. It is the American way to try to be independent. Some of us will not ask for help unless we absolutely have to. If that is you, you are going to have to make a fundamental decision to find your strength in God and not in yourself. None of us are strong enough on our own to fight against the unseen forces of darkness. You will always win, however, if you depend on the strength of the Lord. No one is more powerful than God. It is the power of God that raised Christ from the dead. It is the power of God that brought the world into existence. It is the power of God that is changing your life. If you tap into his power, you cannot lose.

There are two questions you need to answer today. First, will you depend on the Lord for your strength or will you try to do it on your own? What is your decision?.....................

....

What are some ways you depend on yourself rather than God?..

....

Second, are you willing to learn how to fight in the spiritual realm? If you said "yes," the rest of today's guide will help you. Ephesians 6:11 is a summary statement for how to fight and win. First, you must "Put on the full armor of God." You cannot afford to only put on part of the armor of God. You need the full armor of God. You are vulnerable if part of you is exposed because you are missing proper armor.

Being a pastor of a church that is in the same city as one of the largest F-16 bases in the world means I have known lots of soldiers that have fought in the Iraq War. We have lost many men and women in the war. That's a reality of war. What is upsetting is that many of our troops were wounded and killed because they did not have proper armor.[1]

You can be fully protected in spiritual battles. Notice that the word "stand" repeats in Ephesians 6:11, 13 (two times), 14. You can take your stand, resist the attacks of the evil one and not be shaken when you do spiritual warfare, if you put on the full armor of God. You need it all.

Armor Piece #1—The Helmet of Salvation. Accepting the finished work of Christ for you on the cross protects you from fatal head wounds. Take a moment to thank God that he saved you by dying on the cross for your sins. Don't try to work for it, just accept it and thank God now.

Armor Piece #2—The Sword of the Spirit which is the Word of God. The only offensive weapon you have is the Scriptures. Over the next months and years, as you immerse yourself in the Scriptures, you will discover how powerful the Word of God is.

Armor Piece #3—The Belt of Truth. When you know the truth found in the Scriptures, you are no longer vulnerable to the lies of Satan. One of the best questions you can ask yourself when you are tempted is, "What lie am I believing?" When you discover the lie and replace it with the truth expressed in Scripture, you win a battle. I find it fascinating that truth is linked to the middle part of our bodies, the sexual part of our bodies. The truth will affect every area of our lives, especially our sexual behaviors.

Armor Piece #4—The Breastplate of Righteousness. Righteousness is a gift from God that comes by faith in Jesus Christ and it will guard your heart. 2 Corinthians 5:21 states, "God made him who had no sin to be sin for us, so that in him we might become the righteousness of God." Romans 3:22 states, "This righteousness from God comes through faith in Jesus Christ to all who believe." When you trust God to give you righteousness through Jesus, it keeps you from doing things to prove you are righteous. In spiritual warfare, the evil one might bring up your past and tell you how bad or unworthy you are. That is when you remind your enemy and yourself that you are righteous, not because of anything you have done but by faith in Jesus Christ. He makes you righteous. It is a gift, not something you earn.

Armor Piece #5—The Gospel of Peace. Romans 5:1 states, "Therefore, since we have been justified through faith, we have peace with God through our Lord Jesus Christ." You do not need to fear the attack of the evil one in the midst of spiritual warfare because God's peace is with you. Furthermore, there is a reason that peace is linked to your feet. God's peace has an active component to it. You must be prepared to bring God's peace to people who are lost.

Armor Piece #6—The Shield of Faith. A shield is a defensive weapon that keeps you safe from arrows that are sent your way. The evil one does not know your thoughts, but he does know how you acted in past situations. He is a student of your destruction. He will send fiery darts your way in the form of thoughts and opportunities to sin to see if you will accept them and then act on them: hateful thoughts, doubts, a burning desire to sin, a reminder of past hurts, et cetera. When those moments come, your faith in God will keep you from being destroyed. When you are tempted, by faith decide to act on what God's Word says and he will keep you safe.

Armor Piece #7—Praying in the Spirit. Notice how many times prayer is mentioned in Ephesians 6:18–20, "And *pray* in the Spirit on all occasions with all kinds of *prayers* and *requests*. With this in mind, be alert and always keep on *praying* for all the saints. *Pray* also for me, that whenever I open my mouth, words may be given me so that I will fearlessly make known the mystery of the gospel, for which I am an ambassador in chains. *Pray* that I may declare it fearlessly, as I should" (emphasis mine). One of the powerful weapons you have in spiritual battle is prayer, talking with God. There are many different kinds of prayer available to you. Use them all. Praying in the Spirit is praying beyond your mind and words. Have you ever prayed for awhile and run out of words, but you feel like you are not done praying? There are many references in the Bible to people being empowered to pray in a heavenly language they never learned (Acts 2:4, 10:44–45, 19:6; 1 Corinthians 12:10, 12:30, 13:1, 14:1–25). The wonderful thing about praying in the Spirit is that the Spirit of God prays through you. Where your words are inadequate, the Holy Spirit can give you words that adequately express to God what needs to be said. When we pray powerful prayers, powerful things happen. I believe the Bible teaches this experience is available to all believers for private prayer. If you have never heard of this before, you may want to talk about this with your spiritual coach.

Prayer:

Heavenly Father, thank you for giving me the armor and the weapons I need to win in spiritual battle. Teach me how to use each piece of armor and the weapons of spiritual warfare. Enable me to win in battle against the spiritual forces of evil in the heavenly realms. Empower me to pray in the Spirit so I can pray more effectively. I need and want all you have for me. I want to be fully prepared for spiritual battle. Amen.

Attribute Six
Decisions

Attribute Seven

•

Learn to Manage

Attribute Seven • Introduction
Learn to Manage

Read: Deuteronomy 6:4–5

I DIDN'T START FOLLOWING JESUS UNTIL the end of my high school years. As I started to meet to other followers of Jesus, I began to learn what it meant to truly worship God. I thought it was just singing at a service, but it went way beyond that. The greatest commandment in the Bible is to love the LORD our God with all of our heart, with all of our soul, and with all of our strength. This is worship! Giving our best to God and for God is worship and not giving and doing our best is sin. Does that statement change your perspective and future decisions? Your whole life is an opportunity to worship God. We don't do anything to receive his love, but we give our best because he loves us! Loving God involves every area of your life: time, energy, money, influence. Everything. Furthermore, God expects a return on his investment in our lives. God put you and everyone else on the planet at such a time as this, with specific gifts, because he wants and expects each one of us to fulfill a specific purpose for the advancement of his kingdom. Wrapping your head around that will change every decision you make for the rest of your life.

As you take each step, you will look at a different aspect of your life and how to worship God in that aspect of your life: mind, money, body, speech, time. One final suggestion and then we will pray: Remember to focus on loving God as you develop healthy habits. Don't get discouraged as you start to work in these areas. Almost everyone needs support and encouragement as we develop these venues for loving God. This step is just a start. I want to pray for you.

Prayer:
Heavenly Father, thank you so much for loving me and my friends. Your kindness to us is amazing. You have forgiven us of our sins, the things that separated us from you. We are truly grateful. You have given us a hope and a future when we had nothing. As my friends are looking at their resources and how they can love you in everything, I ask you to continue to assure them of your unending love. Encourage them and help them establish good habits as an expression of that love. Lord, you have given us so much. Help us to use it to bring honor to you. In your name we pray, amen.

Attribute Seven • Step One
Manage Your Mind

Scripture Memory (new):

"But seek first his kingdom and his righteousness, and all these things will be given to you as well." Matthew 6:33

Scripture Memory (review):   Matthew 4:19
    Matthew 11:28–30   Matthew 7:24–25
    Matthew 7:7–8   Matthew 28:18–20
    Matthew 22:37–39   Matthew 6:9–13

Read: Philippians 4:8

W E ALREADY TALKED ABOUT THE VERSES right before these verses, Philippians 4:4–7, on Attribute Five–Step 5: how God gives you peace of mind when you rejoice in him always, are gentle to everyone, choose not to be anxious about anything, and pray about everything.

What is the one command in Philippians 4:8? ....

You might be surprised to discover the Greek word for "think" does not simply mean to "think" by trying to exclude other thoughts. It means "to reckon, evaluate, to consider, ponder, let your mind dwell on."[1] What you think about, you will become. What you dwell on is vitally important to your walk with Christ. Put simply, the Apostle Paul is not teaching his readers through this passage to only think about "Christian" books, movies, and music. He is teaching them (and us) to filter what is around you from a Christian perspective. You do this by intentional thinking. 2 Corinthians 10:4–5 reads:

> The weapons we fight with are not the weapons of the world. On the contrary, they have divine power to demolish strongholds. We demolish arguments and every pretension that sets itself up against the knowledge of God, and we take captive every thought to make it obedient to Christ.

To take your thoughts captive you need to notice what you are thinking, and then ask yourself if that thought helps you become obedient to God and his plan for your life. If the thought does not, you must reject it and replace it with the truth as defined by Scripture.

I like Philippians 4:8–9 because it gives a summary about how a spiritually healthy mind thinks. There are things we need to think about. What are they?............................

....

....

When I was in my philosophy classes in college we debated about "truth." What is it? How do you know what it is? Some would say it is subjective or relative. What's true for you might not be true for someone else. Jesus said, "I am the way and the truth and the life" (John 14:6). In other words, Jesus said truth is a person. If you want to know what truth is, you cannot look within yourself. Proverbs 14:12 states, "There is a way that seems right to a man, but in the end it leads to death." Similarly, Jeremiah 17:9 states, "The heart is deceitful above all things and beyond cure. Who can understand it?" Jesus also said in John 17:17, "Sanctify them (the disciples) by the truth; your word is truth." Truth then is God's perspective as exemplified in Jesus and in God's Word.

People who work with money can identify counterfeit money quickly because they work with real money all day long. You will be able to identify what truth is by spending time with Jesus and in his Word.

Is there anything that God says about you or your life that you have a hard time believing?..................................
....

You will want to share this with your spiritual coach so you can have his or her perspective.

What comes to mind when you think "noble?"...............
....

Noble means "honorable, worthy of respect, above reproach." If you are going to think about noble things, you may want to make some decisions about the kinds of movies or television shows you watch. I am not advocating hiding your head in the sand and avoiding what is unpleasant and displeasing. But if you know that the general tenor of a movie or show is not healthy to watch, you do not want to willfully expose yourself to it. There are better things about which to think. Do you need to make any adjustments regarding what you watch?..

The Bible defines "right" as something that conforms to the laws of God and living in accordance to that. In other words, it is right if God says it is right. How might this understanding of "right" affect how you think about something?..
....

Purity refers to moral purity. You are challenged to sort through the media and personal bombardment of sexual promiscuity in our culture and opt for the morally pure. Sexuality is not wrong. For example, it is morally pure to think about a scintillating memory of your spouse. Sexuality is pure within a monogamous marriage. It is not pure to lust after a two-dimensional image on a computer screen of someone who is not your spouse. Do you need to stop thinking some things which are not pure? If so, how will you do that?..

What kinds of things do you need to start thinking about that are pure?

Lovely things are "cheerful, pleasing, and agreeable." They are beautiful. Music, nature, art, athletics can all be "lovely." When you filter life through what is lovely from God's perspective, you find beauty and then thank God for it. How might you dwell on what is truly lovely?

What kinds of things are admirable?

"Excellent" carries with it a sense of quality that includes virtue, morality, and integrity.

"Praiseworthy" means conduct worth talking about that is in keeping with God's moral character.

Read Philippians 4:9. What will happen if you think about these things and model your life after godly people?

There is nothing like having God's peace with you.

What adjustments do you need to make with your thought life?

What can you do to be more intentional about your thought life?

Do you need to stop a certain thought process that is not in keeping with God's will for your life? If so, what is it? How will you do it?

Prayer:

(Thank God for the freedom he offers you to learn how to think his thoughts. Tell God specifically how you intend to make changes in your thought life. Ask God to help you learn how to think in a way that honors him and brings you peace.)

Final thoughts:

I heard this summary about the impact of our thoughts:
Sow a thought, reap an action.
Sow an action, reap a habit.
Sow a habit, reap a character.
Sow a character, reap a destiny![2]

Proverbs 4:23 NCV, "Be careful what you think, because your thoughts run your life."

Attribute Seven • Step Two
Manage Your Money

Scripture Memory:

"But seek ____ his kingdom and ____ righteousness, and ____ these things will be ____ to you as ____." ____ 6:33

"But seek first his kingdom and his righteousness, and all these things will be given to you as well." Matthew 6:33

Read: Matthew 6:19–33

MY MOM AND DAD HAD NOTHING when I was growing up. My dad grew up in the projects in Chicago and his family had nothing. My dad was very skilled, but bounced from job to job in his early twenties. When my parents got divorced and married their new spouses, I could see that my dad wanted his family to have the life he never had. He was a hard worker and did very well. This hard work and desire to provide and to gain was instilled into my life. I wanted to do even better than my family, make lots of money, and have *more*. In fact, my college majors were based on what would make lots of money in life. Even when I became a follower of Jesus I thought I could follow him into being a leader in the church and still make lots of money to make my life even better than what I had growing up.

When I took my first pastoral position at a little country

church in Missouri, for which I got paid $100 a week, I realized that my desire to follow God into being a church leader couldn't be clouded with wanting anything more than Jesus. God began to teach me that he was my provider and that whether I had a lot or a little, my decisions couldn't be made on *wanting*, but on God.

God has provided very well for me and my family, but we have never let our desire be about making money in life. God has provided when I was at the bottom of the barrel and when I felt like I was at the top. I have great joy in knowing that God supplies my needs and he is the center of my life. I want that so much for you, and I know God wants that for you even more.

Jesus addresses this area of your life in Matthew 6:19–33. We already discussed Jesus' warning against storing up for yourself treasures on earth.[1] Your heart will go where you put your treasure. Furthermore, Jesus tells us the truth that we cannot serve God and money (Matthew 6:24).

At this point in your life, would you say that you are serving money?...

If so, what impact does it have on your life?.....................

....

Would you like to make a change in this area of your life? Why or why not?...

....

....

If you decided to make a change, what would that look like for you?...

....

In Matthew 6:25–32, Jesus talks about why worrying is worthless. What are some reasons Jesus gives for why that is so?...

....

....

In Matthew 6:33, what does Jesus tell you to do instead of worrying?...
....

What decision(s) would you like to make based on the truths described in Matthew 6:19–33?............................
....
....
....
....
....
....

I could tell you many stories of God's provision but those are my stories. You need your own stories about what God has done because you surrendered your money to him. You and the Lord can write a new story together of God's faithfulness and miraculous provision. You will never know what that story would have been if you don't surrender. God is amazing. He does all things well. Trust him. Make the decision to follow him with your finances and don't look back. I have never regretted the decision I made to surrender my finances to God. God has blessed me in so many ways because of that. I want that for you, and I know he does as well.

If you would like to know how to take the next practical steps with your finances, there are several places you can go to find great resources.[2] You can also talk with your spiritual coach about this. He or she may have some suggestions for the next steps about how to put God first in your finances.

Prayer:
Heavenly Father, I love you. You have forgiven me of my sins and given me a new life in Christ. You do all things well. I trust you. I make the decision today to

surrender my finances to you. I choose not to serve money any longer. I'm not sure yet what it means but I trust you. Have your way in my finances. Amen.

Attribute Seven • Step Three
Manage Your Body

Scripture Memory:

"But ____ ____ his _____ and ____ _____, and __
these things ___ __ _____ to you as ____." Matthew___:33

---

*"But seek first his kingdom and his righteousness, and all these
things will be given to you as well." Matthew 6:33*

Read: Deuteronomy 6:5; Genesis 1:26–31

GENESIS 1:26–31 CAN HELP YOU REALIGN YOUR LIFE
and how you view your body. There are three things
you must understand from these verses. First, God created
you. You are not self-made. You did not evolve over a long
period of time from an earlier life form. There is a personal,
Creator God who designed you. You are different from anyone who has ever been on this earth. Second, you are made
in God's image. This means you are uniquely designed to
partner with God as his representative in your world for this
time in history. You were not designed to do your own thing.
To get the third point, you need to reread Genesis 1:31. What
did God think about the humans he had made on the sixth
day?..
....

If you look back over Genesis 1 at the end of the other
five days, you will see that God said, "It was good." It was

only after he made humans that God said, "It was *very* good" (emphasis mine). When God looks at you, he sees a masterpiece. The mass media has taught us to compare ourselves to others and to devalue certain aspects of our bodies that are not like someone else's. That is not God's perspective. He made each person different and special. If you are going to become who God has designed you to be, you must allow his thoughts about you to rule. Your body is "very good." You will find great freedom when you look at your body and your life from God's point of view. Why not begin by praying Psalm 139:13–16:

> For you (God) created my inmost being; you knit me together in my mother's womb. I praise you because I am fearfully and wonderfully made; Your works are wonderful, I know that full well. My frame was not hidden from you when I was made in the secret place. When I was woven together in the depths of the earth, your eyes saw my unformed body. All the days ordained for me were written in your book before one of them came to be.

Thanking God for your body and accepting God's view of your body are essential for your walk with God. It is also essential that you accept his purpose for your body, to partner with God for his purpose.

Several Scriptures will help shape how you think about your body. First, Deuteronomy 6:5 describes what you do with your body as worship: "Love the LORD your God with all your heart and with all your soul and with all your strength." Worship is not just what you do on Sunday during a service. Everything you do with your body is an act of worship to God or worship of yourself. In practical terms, what you eat, how much or how little you eat, how much you sleep, what you drink, how and with whom you enjoy sex, how you work, whom you serve and the like, are all matters of worship, ways of expressing your love to God. If you view your body as an instrument to please yourself, you will do

your own thing, what feels good or seems right to you. If you know your body is a gift from God for which you are responsible to him, you will use it to worship him and to bring him honor. Romans 12:1 describes it this way: "Therefore, I urge you, brothers, in view of God's mercy, to offer your bodies as living sacrifices, holy and pleasing to God—this is your spiritual act of worship." Embracing this view of your body will change everything. What comes to your mind right now that you will need to adjust based on the truth of this principle? ....
....

Sometimes when it comes to these kinds of things, people feel like they are going to miss out on a lot of fun. There is no doubt there will be short-term pleasures you will bypass if you offer your body to God. While temporary pleasures like overeating, over drinking, and having sex outside of a monogamous marriage seem to be fun, in the end they produce much pain and disappointment. Overeating results in all kinds of health problems. Alcoholism and drug abuse destroy bodies and families, and they steal valuable resources that could be used to invest in the future. Sex outside of marriage is always destructive. 1 Corinthians 6:18–20 describes it this way:

> Flee sexual immorality. All other sins a man commits are outside his body, but he who sins sexually sins against his own body. Do you not know that your body is a temple of the Holy Spirit, who is in you, whom you have received from God? You are not your own; you were bought at a price. Therefore honor God with your body.

God's ways are always best. Romans 6:12–13 describes the choice you have with your body now that you know the Lord:

> Therefore do not let sin reign in your mortal body so that you obey its evil desires. Do not offer the parts of your body to sin, as instruments of wickedness, but rather offer yourselves

to God, as those who have been brought from death to life; and offer the parts of your body to him as instruments of righteousness.

Adjusting what you do with your body is a process. Most people have to start in one area and then move to another. What aspects of what you do with your body need adjustment? ....

....

....

You will want to prioritize these and strategize with your spiritual coach about what your next decisions need to be.

> **Prayer:**
> Heavenly Father, thank you for my body. I praise you because I am fearfully and wonderfully made. I haven't thought that way about my body until now. Thank you for accepting me and loving me just like I am. Thank you for showing me how much you value my body; you bought me with a precious price. I accept as truth that my body is "very good." I offer my body back to you as an instrument of righteousness. May what I do with my body honor you from this day forward. I need your help as I learn how to do that. Amen.

Attribute Seven • Step Four
Manage Your Words

Scripture Memory:

"But ____ first ____ _____ and ____ _____ , and __
____ _____ ___ __ _____ to ____ as ____." Matthew 6: __

"But seek first his kingdom and his righteousness, and all these things will be given to you as well." Matthew 6:33

Read: James 3:3–12; Matthew 12:33–37; Ephesians 4:29–32

WHEN I WAS A CHILD and someone would say something hurtful, I would often hear my friends say, "Sticks and stones may break my bones but words can never hurt me." We all knew it wasn't true, but they would say it anyway in hopes that the person would stop saying the hurtful things. Words are powerful. We all know it.

What analogies does James use to describe the power of the tongue?...

....

Powerful communication can serve as a rudder to motivate a large group of people to go in a certain direction. It can also destroy lots of people like a spark can destroy a forest. Words are powerful. As a follower of Jesus, your words must become those which turn people to Christ. You may have struggled with your words up till now. Perhaps you have said hurtful things to others or even to yourself. Maybe you gossiped about someone or told a story in a way that made someone look bad. I know I have. As you follow Christ, he will show you how your words can be life-giving.

People do a variety of things to deal with the problem of the tongue. Some people opt to not talk much, just to stuff it. This is not a bad option because it keeps you from saying things you would regret later. Others say things and then try to retract them by saying, "I am sorry I said that. I really didn't mean it. I was just angry." Still others don't worry too much about it. They just say what's on their mind and they let others deal with it. They are proud that people say of them, "You always know where you stand with that person. He speaks his mind." Each of these has their benefits but none of these are the way of Jesus. Let's look at the passages you read today.

According to James 3:5–6, what does the tongue do?......

All three of the responses mentioned above are our attempts to tame our own tongue. What does James 3:8 say about these approaches to the tongue?...............

According to Jesus' words in Matthew 12:33–35, what is the core issue?...............

It really is a heart issue, isn't it? What comes out of you and me is what is really in us. If Christ fills us with good things and removes the bad things in our hearts, our speech will follow because it is out of the overflow of the heart that our mouths speak. If your heart is full of good things, when it overflows, good things will come out. If it is full of evil things, evil things will come out. Think of your tongue as a barometer of your heart. What you talk about and think about is what is important to you. Listen to yourself talk today. What kinds of things do you talk about? You may want to keep a notepad near you today to monitor your thoughts and words. Your words will indicate what you value and the condition of your soul. When you hear yourself saying something you think would not glorify God, ask yourself why you are saying it. Is it because you want others to perceive you a certain way? Are you trying to get someone to do something?

Allowing Jesus to transform your heart and your words is extremely important because Jesus says in Matthew 12:36–37 that we will have to give account one day for every word we said. We are responsible for our hearts and our words. That's a sobering thought. What better time than now to surrender your heart and words to the Lord?

What strategies does the Apostle Paul give in Ephesians 4:29–32 that could help you with your heart and words?..

....

....

If you are going to honor Christ with your tongue, you have to make a concerted effort in five ways. First, even though you cannot tame your tongue, you can curb what you say that is hurtful (Ephesians 4:29). You have probably heard the saying, "If you don't have something good to say, don't say it." There is some truth to this. You can develop the habit of saying only good things about others. Second, you need to acknowledge that it grieves the Holy Spirit when you say hurtful things about others (Ephesians 4:30). God loves everyone, and it hurts him when you talk poorly about the ones he created. Third, you must get rid of bitterness, rage, anger, brawling, slander and malice (Ephesians 4:31). Most of the time we say hurtful things about people who have hurt us. When you want to say something hurtful about someone, ask yourself how that person hurt you. When you identify that hurt, take it to the Lord. You may want to go back to Attribute Six–Step 4 of this guide to remind your-self how to pray through pain. Let God carry the pain for you. Let it go. Get rid of it. Fourth, be kind and compas-sionate to others (Ephesians 6:32). Regardless of how others treat you, you have control over your actions towards them. There is great freedom in knowing someone's actions do not dictate your responses. You can be kind and compassionate towards others because God is that way to you. Fifth, we all need forgiveness. The pathway to learning to love God with your words comes back to God's forgiveness for you. When you remember how much you needed and still need God to forgive you, it enables you to forgive others.

What would you like to do today to apply these prin-ciples to your life?..

....

....

Prayer:
Tell God in your own words what you would like him to help you with today. Be sure to thank him for what he has done in your life already.

Attribute Seven • Step Five
Manage Your Time

Scripture Memory:

"＿＿ ＿＿ ＿＿ ＿＿ ＿＿＿＿ ＿＿ ＿＿ ＿＿＿＿＿ , ＿＿ ＿＿
＿＿ ＿＿ ＿＿ ＿＿ ＿ ＿ ＿ ＿ ＿ ＿." ＿＿＿＿ ＿ : ＿

"But seek first his kingdom and his righteousness, and all these things will be given to you as well." Matthew 6:33

Read: Genesis 2:2–3; Exodus 20:8–11; Genesis 2:15; Psalm 90:12; Ecclesiastes 3

LEO TOLSTOY WROTE A FAMOUS STORY entitled, "How Much Land Does a Man Need?"[1] In it he describes an ambitious peasant named Pakhom, who heard about a country where he could have all the land he wanted for a thousand rubles. The only requirement was that he had to be able to walk around the entire plot in one day. Pakhom was quite confident that he could go far in one day. The rules were simple. He paid the thousand rubles upfront, would walk the entire property in one day, and then return to the starting point by sundown. If he did not get back to the starting point by sundown, the money and the land would be forfeited. In the story, Pakhom went too far in the early part of the day which resulted in his having to push himself especially hard to try to get back to the starting point. Near the end of the day the story describes him running with burning lungs, a sweat-soaked shirt and a parched throat. He did make it back to the starting point just in time and he collapsed. Pakhom's worker ran to help him up only to discover he had died of exhaustion. The worker took Pakhom's shovel, dug a grave, and buried him on a six-foot piece of land, the exact amount of land a man needs.

Many of us are running ourselves ragged by living overloaded lives. Our lust for more is driving us to live beyond our limits, and it is resulting in exhaustion and burnout.[2] God did not design us to work or play all the time. He designed us to work hard for short seasons and then to rest and reflect.

God set aside one day a week for rest and renewal. Read Genesis 2:2–3 again. Does it surprise you that God rested from his work? Why or why not?

I believe God rested on the seventh day not because he was tired but to model for us that we need it.

God's ways are always best but we don't always think so. Notice in Exodus 20:7–11 that taking a Sabbath is one of the Ten Commandments. God requires it of his people.

Why do you think most Americans do not take a day to rest and reflect?..

Do you currently take a day to rest and reflect? Why or why not?..

....

Some people start obeying God in this area by taking a portion of a day to rest and reflect and then grow into it. Others just dive right in and take twenty-four hours. Would you like to work towards taking a Sabbath (one day to rest) or a portion of a Sabbath?..

....

What kinds of things could you do on a Sabbath to help you renew your spiritual, physical, and emotional being?..

What decisions would you need to make for that to happen?..

What will you have to give up?..

Choosing to not work when you are able is equally dishonoring to God. Notice in Genesis 2:15 that God gave man work before the curse. In other words, work is not part of the curse. Work is harder because of the curse but work is not the curse. This means it is God's will that you would embrace your work in life. The Bible describes those who do not work faithfully as "sluggards." There are painful consequences for living the life of a sluggard which you will want to avoid.[3] The Apostle Paul wrote directly to men in 1 Timothy 5:8 about providing for their families, "If anyone does not provide for his relatives, and especially for his immediate family, he has denied the faith and is worse than an unbeliever."

Is working a problem for you?..

If so, what step are you going to take to change this?........

....

Learning to be a good manager of your time is all about balance, making sure you are taking care of the most important things first. A good start is to establish times when you work and rest and reflect. We could have also talked about making time for important relationships, taking care of your body, et cetera. It is a process to learn how to use your time to honor God.

Are there other areas of your life that you need God's help with concerning your time?..

....

What needs to happen so you can take steps in the right direction?..
....

You will want to share your decisions with your spiritual coach.

How about asking God to help you right now by praying Psalm 90:12 with the psalmist?

> ***Prayer:***
> Lord, teach me to number my days aright, that I may gain a heart of wisdom. I want to please you with how I manage my time. Help me as I take steps today to be faithful with the time you have given me. I want to honor you and fulfill my purpose. I believe I can do that if you will help me and guide me. Amen.

Attribute Seven • Step Six
Manage Your Gifts

Scripture Memory:

" ___ ___ ___ ___ ___ ___ ___ ___ , ___ ___

___ ___ ___ ___ ___ ___ ___ ___ ." ___ ___ : ___

"But seek first his kingdom and his righteousness, and all these things will be given to you as well." Matthew 6:33

Read: Ephesians 2:10; 1 Corinthians 12:7–11; 1 Peter 4:10–11; Matthew 25:14–30

IT IS AN AMAZING THING TO ME THAT GOD ALLOWS US the privilege of joining with him to change the world. He could do everything himself, but he chooses to do some of his work through us. I am so humbled by that.

How does Ephesians 2:10 describe us? ....

....

Why were we created? ....

When did God prepare our work for us? ....

....

You are not an accident or an evolution of nature. God had you in mind long before you were born. He designed you with specific spiritual gifts, passions, abilities, and a certain personality type so you could make a unique impact on the world that would bring him glory. Isn't that affirming? You may not know at this point what your unique contribution will be for God, but the Bible assures you that God has a plan for your life that is unlike anyone else's.

According to 1 Corinthians 12:7, to whom does the Spirit give gifts? ....

....

Why were these gifts given? ....

It is really important to realize the gifts God gives you are not for you but for others. No one has all the gifts. That's why we need one another to become all that God wants us to become. When I do my part and you do yours, we can make an impact for God.

According to 1 Corinthians 12:11, who decides who receives which gifts?

How does 1 Peter 4:10 affect how you think about your gifts? ....

....

According to 1 Peter 4:11, what is the ultimate goal of your gifts? ....

....

I would not be telling you the whole truth if I didn't tell you there are huge implications for how you manage the gifts God has given you. Matthew 25:14–30 describes God's kingdom like a master who entrusted his property to his servants before he went on a journey. He gave each of them a different portion of his property (called "talents" in the story). When he returned, he expected each of them to have done something with the resources he gave them. Those who received five and two talents used them to gain even more. This pleased the master and he put them in charge of many things. But the servant who received only one talent and did nothing with it, received a harsh rebuke from the master. The master said, "You wicked, lazy servant." And the master took what he had given to that servant, and he gave it away to those who had done something with their resources. Then the master cast the servant out into the darkness where there was weeping and gnashing of teeth. This is a sobering parable but one we should take to heart as followers of Jesus. God invests heavily in each one of us because he has significant purposes for our lives. His purpose for your life is important. You only fail if you attempt nothing for God.

What gifts and resources has God given you?................

....

....

What would you like to do for God if you knew he would bless it?...

....

....

What could you do with what God has given you to serve others? ....

....

....

As we conclude *Learning to Follow Jesus*, I want to pray for us.

> **Prayer:**
> It amazes me, Heavenly Father, that you reach out to us to show us your kindness, to love us, to teach us, to befriend us, and to give us a meaningful life. It humbles me to realize that our lives matter so much to you. Help us to manage the gifts and resources you have given us in such a way that we fulfill what you had in mind when you created us. Help us to live today and each day hereafter for you alone. Thank you for giving our lives meaning. We belong to you. Amen.

Attribute Seven
Decisions

Resources

Attribute One • Learn to Be With Jesus
Resources

How to Develop a Schedule

1. Values

+ The values of the follower of Jesus are two-fold: loving God and loving people.

2. Roles

+ God has given you specific roles (steward, husband, father, friend, et cetera) and resources to manage (time, talent, energy, and money).

3. Tasks

+ Make a list of tasks you perform under each role.

4. Time

+ Estimate the amount of time each task will take on a weekly basis so that Christ is honored.

+ Add up the hours and subtract the total from 168.

5. Analysis

+ Set aside time weekly to evaluate and plan how you will spend your time based on your values.

6. **Plot** the hours on a weekly schedule.

Sample Time Analysis

1. LOVER OF GOD (135.5 hours)	Wkly Hrs	Total
a. Steward—Spiritual Formation		11
i. Quiet time—30 mins x 7 days	3.5	
ii. Corporate Worship Service	2.5	
iii. Small Group/with dinner	3	
iv. Spiritual Coach—1 hr	1	
v. Ministry Involvement	1	
b. Steward—Physical, Emotional, Mental		74.5
i. Sleep (8 hours)	56	
ii. Eating (Breakfast .5; Lunch .5)	7	
iii. Personal hygiene (30 minutes daily)	4.5	
iv. Workout—Cardio/reading	3	
v. Reading	3	
vi. Weekly planning	1	
c. Steward - Employment		50
i. Work	45	
ii. Commuting Time	5	
2. LOVER OF PEOPLE (32 hours)		
a. Spouse		10
i. Personal Time	7	
ii. Household Chores	3	
b. Father		16
i. Dinner	6	
ii. Family Time	7	
iii. Family Night	3	
c. Friends, Neighbors, & Extended Family		6
i. Neighbors	1	
ii. Friendship with a pre-Christian	1	
iii. Friendship—social networking, activities	4	
TOTAL HOURS		167.5
TOTAL HOURS IN A WEEK		168
TOTAL AVAILABLE TIME		.5

Attribute Two • Learn to Listen
Resources

Bible Study Process

Choose a **Passage** (usually a paragraph) of Scripture you would like to study (I recommend starting with Philippians 4:4–7).

Step 1—Read through the entire **Book** in which your passage occurs in no more than two sittings. Take note of what stands out to you. What questions do you have as you read the book?

Step 2—Reread the entire **Book** looking for clues to the following questions: Who wrote the book? To whom did he write? What kinds of issues were important to the recipients? Are there any clues in the book as to when the letter was written? Why was the book written? What are the natural or logical divisions of the book?

Step 3—Read what others say about the 5 questions in Bible dictionaries, Bible encyclopedias, Bible handbooks, commentaries, and introductions.

Step 4—Identify the **Section** of the book in which your **Passage** occurs. (A **Section** is a group of **Passages** [paragraphs] that have the same focus.) Read the **Section** twice and identify the following:
 1. The main focus of your **Section** in one sentence.
 2. How each **Passage** advances the main focus of your **Section**.

Step 5—Read your **Passage** 3 times. List as many observations as you can about your **Passage** using the six observation questions to guide you: What is emphasized? What is repeated? What is related? What is alike? What is unlike? What is true to life?

Step 6—Read your **Passage** in 4 different translations and look up all marginal references in your passage.

Step 7—Identify, research, and explain every historical context item in your **Passage**.

Step 8—Do the following steps for every significant word in your **Passage:**
1. Where does this word occur in the passage? First sentence? Last?
2. Is the word repeated in the passage? If so, how many times and in which verse(s)?
3. At first glance what do you think this word means in this passage?
4. Using a concordance, make a list of every reference to your word in the book you are studying.
5. Look up and read every reference to the word in the book. (Note: if the word is used more than 25–30 times in the book, look up primarily those which fall in your section and others which seem to be significant throughout the book.)
6. Write a short phrase beside each reference to help you remember the context. (Note: if you are studying a verb, include who is speaking or doing the action and to whom. In what context is the action taking place? If you are studying a noun, what is this thing used for? If it is a place, what happens there?)
7. Is this word used in similar contexts? What is that context?
8. Does the word occur primarily in one section or passage of the book?
9. Read about your word from theological wordbooks and commentaries.

10.How does the meaning of this word clarify the meaning of the sentence in the passage in the section in the book you are studying?

Step 9—Develop a one-sentence statement that includes the main idea of the **Passage** and what it meant to the original audience.

Step 10—Develop a one sentence teaching statement that summarizes what the **Passage** means for all people. How will people's lives change if they get the main point of this passage? What will people think, feel, and do if they get the point?

Attribute Three • Learn to Heal
Resources

Conflict Resolution Process[1]

Overview of Conflict
1. It is a normal part of life.
2. Provides an opportunity to grow.
3. We decide how we are going to handle conflict.

Problem Solving Process
1. Pray to get your own heart right before you do anything.
   → Do not proceed until you know before God that you love the other person and want God's best for them.
2. Set a time and place for discussion
   → Make sure you set aside adequate time.
   → Choose a place to talk where you will not be interrupted.
3. Define the problem or issue of disagreement.
   → Select one issue at a time.

    ⇾ Define the issue in a way that is mutually agreeable.
4. How do each of you contribute to the problem?
    ⇾ The purpose is to discover how the problem evolved in order to find a solution.
5. List past attempts to resolve the issue that were not successful.
6. Brainstorm about possible solutions.
    ⇾ The purpose of this is to generate fresh ideas without attempting to evaluate their relative merits.
7. Discuss and evaluate the possible solutions.
8. Agree on one solution and try.
    ⇾ To agree upon a choice does not always mean it is the first choice of either partner.
9. Agree on how each individual will work toward this solution.
    ⇾ Be specific and focus on observable behaviors.
10. Set up another meeting to discuss your progress.
    ⇾ Set the meeting reasonably soon (i.e., one week from now).
    ⇾ Partners can discuss the degree to which the plan is working and in which to further their progress.
11. Reward each other as you each contribute toward the solution.
    ⇾ Watch for ways in which your partner positively contributes to resolving the conflict.
    ⇾ Encourage and praise one another for their efforts.

Grief Process[2]

1. **Shock stage:** Initial paralysis at hearing the bad news.
2. **Denial stage:** Frustrated outpouring of bottled-up emotion.

3. **Bargaining stage:** Seeking in vain for a way out.
4. **Depression stage:** Final realization of the inevitable.
5. **Testing stage:** Seeking realistic solutions.
6. **Acceptance stage:** Finally finding the way forward.

12 Step Recovery Process with Scripture References[3]

Step 1 We admitted we were powerless over our addictions and compulsive behaviors, that our lives had become unmanageable.

> I know that nothing good lives in me, that is, in my sinful nature. For I have the desire to do what is good, but I cannot carry it out. Romans 7:18

Step 2 We came to believe that a power greater than ourselves could restore us to sanity.

> For it is God who works in you to will and to act according to his good purpose. Philippians 2:13

Step 3 We made a decision to turn our lives and our wills over to the care of God.

> Therefore, I urge you, brothers, in view of God's mercy, to offer your bodies as living sacrifices, holy and pleasing to God—this is your spiritual act of worship. Romans 12:1

Step 4 We made a searching and fearless moral inventory of ourselves.

> Let us examine our ways and test them, and let us return to the Lord. Lamentations 3:40

Step 5 We admitted to God, to ourselves, and to another human being the exact nature of our wrongs.

> Therefore confess your sins to each other and pray for each other so that you may be healed. James 5:16

Step 6 We were entirely ready to have God remove all these defects of character.

> Humble yourselves before the Lord, and he will lift you up. James 4:10

Step 7 We humbly asked Him to remove all our shortcomings.

> If we confess our sins, he is faithful and just and will forgive us our sins and purify us from all unrighteousness. 1 John 1:9

Step 8 We made a list of all persons we had harmed and became willing to make amends to them all.

> Do to others as you would have them do to you. Luke 6:31

Step 9 We made direct amends to such people whenever possible, except when to do so would injure them or others.

> Therefore, if you are offering your gift at the altar and there remember that your brother has something against you, leave your gift there in front of the altar. First go and be reconciled to your brother; then come and offer your gift. Matthew 5:23–24

Step 10 We continue to take personal inventory and when we were wrong, promptly admitted it.

> So, if you think you are standing firm, be careful that you don't fall! 1 Corinthians 10:12

Step 11 We sought through prayer and meditation to improve our conscious contact with God, praying only for knowledge of his will for us, and power to carry that out.

> Let the word of Christ dwell in you richly. Colossians 3:16

Step 12 Having had a spiritual experience as the result of these steps, we try to carry this message to others and to practice these principles in all our affairs.

> Brothers, if someone is caught in a sin, you who are spiritual should restore him gently. But watch yourself, or you also may be tempted. Galatians 6:1

4 Attribute Four • Learn to Influence
Resources

Evangelism Styles Questionnaire[1]

Directions

1. Record your response to each of the 36 statements according to whether you think that statement applies to you:

3	2	1	0
Very much	Somewhat	Very little	Not at all

2. Transfer your responses to the grid at the bottom of page 222 and total each column.

........1. In conversations, I like to approach topics directly, without much small talk or beating around the bush.

........2. I have a hard time getting out of bookstores or libraries without getting a bunch of books that will help me better understand issues being debated in society.

........3. I often tell stories about my personal experiences in order to illustrate a point I am trying to make.

........4. I am a "people person" who places a high value on friendship.

........5. I enjoy including or adding new people to activities in which I am involved.

........6. I see needs in people's lives that others often overlook.

........7. I do not shy away from putting a person on the spot when it seems necessary.

........8. I tend to be analytical.

........9. I often identify with others by using phrases like "I used to think that too" or "I once felt the way you do."

.......10. Other people have commented about my ability for developing new friendships.

.......11. To be honest, even if I know the answers, I am more comfortable having someone "better qualified" explain Christianity to my friends.

.......12. I find fulfillment in helping others, often in behind-the-scenes ways.

......13. I do not have a problem confronting my friends with the truth even if it risks hurting the relationship.

......14. In conversations, I naturally focus on the questions that are holding up a person's spiritual progress.

......15. When I tell people how I came to Christ, I have found that they have been interested in hearing it.

......16. I would rather delve into personal life issues than abstract theological ideas.

......17. If I knew of a high quality outreach event that my friends would enjoy, I would make a big effort to bring them.

......18. I prefer to show love through my actions more than my words.

......19. I believe that real love often means telling someone the truth, even when it hurts.

......20. I enjoy discussions and debates on difficult questions.

......21. I intentionally share my mistakes with others when it will help them relate to the solutions I have found.

......22. I prefer getting involved in discussions concerning a person's life before dealing with the details of their beliefs.

......23. I tend to watch for spiritually strategic events to bring people to (such as Christian concerts, outreach events, seeker services).

......24. When people are spiritually closed, I have found that my quiet demonstrations of Christian love sometimes make them more receptive.

......25. A motto that would fit me is: "Make a difference or a mess, but do something."

......26. I often get frustrated with people when they use weak arguments or poor logic.

......27. People seem interested in hearing stories about things that have happened in my life.

......28. I enjoy long talks with friends.

......29. I am always looking for a match between the needs and interests of my friends and the various events, books, etc., that they would enjoy or from which they would benefit.

......30. I feel more comfortable physically assisting a person in the name of Christ than getting involved in religious discussions.

........31. I sometimes get in trouble for lacking gentleness and sensitivity in the way I interact with others.

........32. I like to get at the underlying reasons for opinions people hold.

........33. I am still amazed at how God brought me to faith in Him and I am motivated to tell people about it.

........34. People generally consider me to be an interactive, sensitive, and caring kind of person.

........35. A highlight of my week would be to take a guest with me to an appropriate church event.

........36. I tend to be more practical and action-oriented than philosophical and idea-oriented.

	Confrontational	Intellectual	Testimonial	Interpersonal	Invitational	Serving
	#1 ___	#2 ___	#3 ___	#4 ___	#5 ___	#6 ___
	#7 ___	#8 ___	#9 ___	#10 ___	#11 ___	#12 ___
	#13 ___	#14 ___	#15 ___	#16 ___	#17 ___	#18 ___
	#19 ___	#20 ___	#21 ___	#22 ___	#23 ___	#24 ___
	#25 ___	#26 ___	#27 ___	#28 ___	#29 ___	#30 ___
	#31 ___	#32 ___	#33 ___	#34 ___	#35 ___	#36 ___
TOTALS						

Evangelism Style Examples & Summaries

Confrontational Style—Acts 2—Peter, Billy Graham, Chuck Colson
- ✦ Characteristics: Confident, Assertive, Direct
- ✦ Cautions: Be sure to use tact when confronting people with truth to keep them from becoming unnecessarily offended.

Intellectual Style—Acts 17—Paul, Josh McDowell, D. James Kennedy, Alpha Course

+ Characteristics: Inquisitive, Analytical, Logical
+ Cautions: Do not substitute giving answers for giving the Gospel message. Be careful of becoming argumentative.

Testimonial Style—John 9:25—Blind man, Corrie ten Boom, Joni Erickson Tada
+ Characteristics: Clear Communicator, Story Teller, Good Listener
+ Cautions: Beware of talking about yourself but not relating your experience to the other person's life. You first need to listen to them to be able to connect your story to their situation.

Interpersonal Style—Luke 5:29—Matthew, Becky Pippert, Joe Aldrich
+ Characteristics: Warm Personality, Conversational, Friendship-Oriented
+ Cautions: Avoid valuing friendship over truth-telling. Presenting the Gospel often means challenging a person's whole direction in life, and that can mean causing friction in your relationship.

Invitational Style—John 1:42, 46—Andrew & Philip, woman at the well in John 4, Ruth Graham
+ Characteristics: Hospitable, Relational, Persuasive
+ Cautions: Be careful not to always let others do your talking for you. You too, need to "always be prepared to give an answer to everyone who asks you to give the reason for the hope that you have..." (1 Peter 3:15)

Serving Style—Acts 9—Dorcas, Mother Teresa
+ Characteristics: Others-Centered, Humble, Patient
+ Cautions: Just as "words are no substitute for actions," "actions are no substitute for words." In Romans 10:14, it is made clear that we verbally tell people about Christ.

Attribute Five • Learn to Love
Resources
Step 1–Trusting God Assessment[1]
Instructions

1. Read each of the following statements and put the appropriate number of the term that best describes you.

2. Add up the total number for each section.

3. Read the interpretation of your score that is found on the next page.

1	2	3	4	5	6	7
Always	Very Often	Often	Sometimes	Seldom	Very Seldom	Never

........1. Because of fear, I often avoid participating in certain activities.

........2. When I sense that I might experience failure in some important area, I become nervous and anxious.

........3. I worry.

........4. I have unexplained anxiety.

........5. I am a perfectionist.

........6. I am compelled to justify my mistakes.

........7. There are certain areas in which I feel I *must* succeed.

........8. I become depressed when I fail.

........9. I am angry with people who interfere with my attempts to succeed, and as a result, make me appear incompetent.

........10. I am self-critical.

........TOTAL (See next page for analysis.)

Trusting God versus Fear of Failure

If your score is...

57–70: God has apparently given you a very strong appreciation for His love and unconditional acceptance. You seem to be freed from the fear of failure that plagues most people. (Some people who score this high are either greatly deceived, or have become callous to their emotions as a way to suppress pain.)

47–56: The fear of failure controls your responses rarely, or only in certain situations. Again, the only major exceptions are those who are not honest with themselves.

37–46: When you experience emotional problems, they may relate to a sense of failure or to some form of criticism. Upon reflection, you will probably relate many of your previous decisions to this fear. Many of your future decisions will also be affected by the fear of failure unless you take direct action to overcome it.

27–36: The fear of failure forms a general backdrop to your life. There are probably few days that you are not affected in some way by this fear. Unfortunately, this robs you of the joy and peace your salvation is meant to bring.

0–26: Experiences of failure dominate your memory, and have probably resulted in a great deal of depression. These problems will remain until some definitive action is taken. In other words, this condition will not simply disappear; time alone cannot heal your pain. You need to experience deep healing in your self-concept, in your relationship with God, and in your relationships with others.

Step 2—Seeking God Assessment[2]
Instructions

1. Read each of the following statements and put the appropriate number of the term that best describes you.

2. Add up the total number for each section.

3. Read the interpretation of your score that is found on the next page.

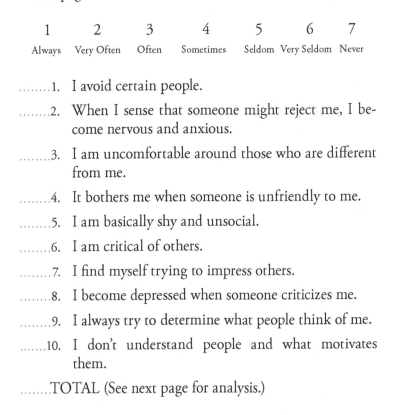

1	2	3	4	5	6	7
Always	Very Often	Often	Sometimes	Seldom	Very Seldom	Never

........1.   I avoid certain people.

........2.   When I sense that someone might reject me, I become nervous and anxious.

........3.   I am uncomfortable around those who are different from me.

........4.   It bothers me when someone is unfriendly to me.

........5.   I am basically shy and unsocial.

........6.   I am critical of others.

........7.   I find myself trying to impress others.

........8.   I become depressed when someone criticizes me.

........9.   I always try to determine what people think of me.

........10. I don't understand people and what motivates them.

........TOTAL (See next page for analysis.)

Seeking God's Approval versus Fear of Rejection

If your score is...

57–70: God has apparently given you a very strong appreciation for His love and unconditional acceptance. You seem to be freed from the fear of rejection that plagues most people. (Some people who score this high are either greatly deceived, or have become callous to their emotions as a way to suppress pain.)

47–56: The fear of rejection controls your responses rarely, or only in certain situations. Again, the only major exceptions are those who are not honest with themselves.

37–46: When you experience emotional problems, they may relate to a sense of rejection. Upon reflection, you will probably relate many of your previous decisions to this fear. Many of your future decisions will also be affected by the fear of rejection unless you take direct action to overcome it.

27–36: The fear of rejection forms a general backdrop to your life. There are probably few days that you are not affected in some way by this fear. Unfortunately, this robs you of the joy and peace your salvation is meant to bring.

0–26: Experiences of rejection dominate your memory, and have probably resulted in a great deal of depression. These problems will persist until some definitive action is taken. In other words, this condition will not simply disappear; time alone cannot heal your pain. You need to experience deep healing in your self-concept, in your relationship with God, and in your relationships with others.

Step 3—Enjoying God's Acceptance Assessment[3]
Instructions

1. Read each of the following statements and put the appropriate number of the term that best describes you.

2. Add up the total number for each section.

3. Read the interpretation of your score that is found on the next page.

1	2	3	4	5	6	7
Always	Very Often	Often	Sometimes	Seldom	Very Seldom	Never

.........1. I fear what God might do to me.

.........2. After I fail, I worry about God's response.

.........3. When I see someone in a difficult situation, I wonder what he or she did to deserve it.

.........4. When something goes wrong, I have a tendency to think that God must be punishing me.

.........5. I am very hard on myself when I fail.

.........6. I find myself wanting to blame people when they fail.

.........7. I get angry with God when someone who is immoral or dishonest prospers.

.........8. I am compelled to tell others when I see them doing wrong.

.........9. I tend to focus on the faults and failures of others.

.........10. God seems harsh to me.

.........TOTAL (See next page for analysis.)

Enjoying God's Acceptance versus Fear of Punishment

If your score is...

57–70: God has apparently given you a very strong appreciation for His unconditional love and acceptance. You seem to be freed from the fear of punishment that plagues most people. (Some people who score this high are either greatly deceived, or have become callous to their emotions as a way to suppress pain.)

47–56: The fear of punishment and the compulsion to punish others controls your responses rarely, or only in certain situations. Again, the only major exceptions are those who are not honest with themselves.

37–46: When you experience emotional problems, they may relate to a fear of punishment or to an inner urge to punish others. Upon reflection, you will probably relate many of your previous decisions to this fear. Many of your future decisions will also be affected by the fear of punishment and/or the compulsion to punish others unless you take direct action to overcome these tendencies.

27–36: The fear of punishment forms a general backdrop to your life. There are probably few days that you are not affected in some way by the fear of punishment and the propensity to blame others. Unfortunately, this robs you of the joy and peace your salvation is meant to bring.

0–26: Experiences of punishment dominate your memory, and you probably have suffered a great deal of depression as a result of them. These problems will remain until some definitive plan is followed. In other words, this condition will not simply disappear; time alone cannot heal your pain. You need to experience deep healing in your self-concept, in your relationship with God, and in your relationships with others.

Step 4—Partnering with God to Change You Assessment[4]
Instructions

1.Read each of the following statements and put the appropriate number of the term that best describes you.

2.Add up the total number for each section.

3.Read the interpretation of your score that is found on the next page.

1	2	3	4	5	6	7
Always	Very Often	Often	Sometimes	Seldom	Very Seldom	Never

........1. I often think about past failures or experiences of rejection.

........2. There are certain things about my past which I cannot recall without experiencing strong, painful emotions (i.e. guilt, shame, anger, fear, etc.).

........3. I seem to make the same mistakes over and over again.

........4. There are certain aspects of my character that I want to change, but I don't believe I can ever successfully do so.

........5. I feel inferior.

........6. There are aspects of my appearance that I cannot accept.

........7. I am generally disgusted with myself.

........8. I feel that certain experiences have basically ruined my life.

........9. I perceive of myself as an immoral person.

.......10. I feel that I have lost the opportunity to experience a complete and wonderful life.

........TOTAL (See next page for analysis.)

Partnering with God for Change versus Fear of Shame

If your score is...

57–70: God has apparently given you a very strong appreciation for His love and unconditional acceptance. You seem to be freed from the shame that plagues most people. (Some people who score this high are either greatly deceived, or have become callous to their emotions as a way to suppress pain.)

47–56: Shame controls your responses rarely, or only in certain situations. Again, the exceptions are those who are not honest with themselves.

37–46: When you experience emotional problems, they may relate to a sense of shame. Upon reflection, you will probably relate many of your previous decisions to feelings of worthlessness. Many of your future decisions will also be affected by low self-esteem unless you take direct action to overcome it.

27–36: Shame forms a generally negative backdrop to your life. There are probably few days that you are not affected in some way by shame. Unfortunately, this robs you of the joy and peace your salvation was meant to bring.

0–26: Experiences of shame dominate your memory, and have probably resulted in a great deal of depression. These problems will persist until some definitive action is taken. In other words, this condition will not simply disappear one day; time alone cannot heal your pain. You need to experience deep healing in your self-concept, in your relationship with God, and in your relationships with others.

God's Answer for Four Common Lies[5]

Lie	False Beliefs
The Performance Trap	I must meet certain standards in order to feel good about myself.
Approval Addict	I must be approved (accepted) by certain others to feel good about myself.
The Blame Game	Those who fail are unworthy of love and deserve to be punished.
Shame	I am what I am. I cannot change. I am hopeless.

Consequences	God's Answer
The fear of failure; perfectionism; driven to succeed; manipulating others to achieve success; withdrawal from risks.	**Justification** Justification means that God has not only forgiven me of my sins, but also has granted me the righteousness of Christ. Because of justification, I bear Christ's righteousness and am, therefore, fully pleasing to the Father (Rom. 5:1).
The fear of rejection; attempting to please others at any cost; overly sensitive to criticism; withdrawing from others to avoid disapproval.	**Reconciliation** Reconciliation means that although I was at one time hostile toward God and alienated from Him, I am now forgiven and have been brought into an intimate relationship with Him. Consequently, I am totally accepted by God (Col. 1:21–22).
The fear of punishment; punishing others; blaming others for personal failure; withdrawal from God and others; driven to avoid failure.	**Propitiation** Propitiation means that Christ satisfied God's wrath by His death on the cross; therefore, I am deeply loved by God (1 John 4:9–11).
Feelings of shame, hopelessness, inferiority; passivity; loss of creativity; isolation; withdrawal from others.	**Regeneration** Regeneration means that I am a new creation in Christ (John 3:3–6).

General
Resources

Who Does God Say I Am?

+ **I am a child of God.**

    Yet to all who received him, to those who believed in his name, he gave the right to become children of God. (John 1:12)

+ **I am a branch of the true vine, and a conduit of Christ's life.**

    I am the true vine, and my Father is the gardener...I am the vine; you are the branches. If a man remains in me and I in him, he will bear much fruit; apart from me you can do nothing. (John 15:1, 5)

+ **I am a friend of Jesus.**

    I no longer call you servants, because a servant does not know his master's business. Instead, I have called you friends, for everything that I learned from my Father I have made known to you. (John 15:15)

+ **I am justified and redeemed.**

    This righteousness from God comes through faith in Jesus Christ to all who believe. There is no difference, for all have sinned and fall short of the glory of God, and are justified freely by his grace through the redemption that came by Christ Jesus. (Romans 3:22-24)

+ **My old self was crucified with Christ, and I am no longer a slave to sin.**

    For we know that our old self was crucified with him so that the body of sin might be done away with, that we should no longer be slaves to sin—because anyone who has died has been freed from sin. (Romans 6:6-7)

+ **God will not condemn me.**

    Therefore, there is now no condemnation for those who are in Christ Jesus...(Romans 8:1)

- I am set free from the law of sin and death.

  For through Christ Jesus the law of the Spirit of life set me free from the law of sin and death. (Romans 8:2)

- As a child of God, I am a fellow heir with Christ.

  Now if we are children, then we are heirs—heirs of God and co-heirs with Christ, if indeed we share in his sufferings in order that we may also share in his glory. (Romans 8:17)

- Christ accepts me.

  Accept one another, then, just as Christ accepted you, in order to bring praise to God. (Romans 15:7)

- I am called to be a saint.

  To the church of God in Corinth, to those sanctified in Christ Jesus and called to be holy, together with all those everywhere who call on the name of our Lord Jesus Christ—their Lord and ours. (1 Corinthians 1:2; see also Ephesians 1:1; Philippians 1:1; Colossians 1:2)

- In Christ Jesus, I have wisdom, righteousness, sanctification, and redemption.

  It is because of him that you are in Christ Jesus, who has become for us wisdom from God—that is, our righteousness, holiness and redemption. (1 Corinthians 1:30)

- My body is the temple of the Holy Spirit, who dwells in me.

  Don't you know that you yourselves are God's temple and that God's Spirit lives in you?...Do you not know that your body is a temple of the Holy Spirit, who is in you, whom you have received from God? You are not your own; you were bought at a price. Therefore honor God with your body. (1 Corinthians 3:16; 6:19–20)

- I am joined to the Lord and am one in spirit with him.

  But he who unites himself with the Lord is one with him in spirit. (1 Corinthians 6:17)

- **God leads me in the triumph and knowledge of Christ.**

  But thanks be to God, who always leads us in triumphal procession in Christ and through us spreads everywhere the fragrance of the knowledge of him. (2 Corinthians 2:14)

- **The hardening of my mind has been removed in Christ.**

  But their minds were made dull, for to this day the same veil remains when the old covenant is read. It has not been removed, because only in Christ is it taken away. (2 Corinthians 3:14)

- **I am a new creature in Christ.**

  Therefore, if anyone is in Christ, he is a new creation; the old has gone, the new has come! (2 Corinthians 5:17)

- **I have become the righteousness of God in Christ.**

  God made him who had no sin to be sin for us, so that in him we might become the righteousness of God. (2 Corinthians 5:21)

- **I have been made one with all who are in Christ Jesus.**

  There is neither Jew nor Greek, slave nor free, male nor female, for you are all one in Christ Jesus. (Galatians 3:28)

- **I am no longer a slave but a child and an heir.**

  So you are no longer a slave, but a son; and since you are a son, God has made you also an heir. (Galatians 4:7)

- **I have been set free in Christ.**

  It is for freedom that Christ has set us free. Stand firm, then, and do not let yourselves be burdened again by a yoke of slavery. (Galatians 5:1)

- **I have been blessed with every spiritual blessing in the heavenly places.**

  Praise be to the God and Father of our Lord Jesus Christ, who has blessed us in the heavenly realms with every spiritual blessing in Christ. (Ephesians 1:3)

◆ **I am chosen, holy, and blameless before God.**

For he chose us in him before the creation of the world to be holy and blameless in his sight. (Ephesians 1:4)

◆ **I am redeemed and forgiven by the grace of Christ.**

In him we have redemption through his blood, the forgiveness of sins, in accordance with the riches of God's grace... (Ephesians 1:7)

◆ **I have been predestined by God to obtain an inheritance.**

To be put into effect when the times will have reached their fulfillment—to bring all things in heaven and on earth together under one head, even Christ. In him we were also chosen, having been predestined according to the plan of him who works out everything in conformity with the purpose of his will...(Ephesians 1:10-11)

◆ **I have been sealed with the Holy Spirit of promise.**

And you also were included in Christ when you heard the word of truth, the gospel of your salvation. Having believed, you were marked in him with a seal, the promised Holy Spirit... (Ephesians 1:13)

◆ **Because of God's mercy and love, I have been made alive with Christ.**

But because of his great love for us, God, who is rich in mercy, made us alive with Christ even when we were dead in transgressions—it is by grace you have been saved. (Ephesians 2:4-5)

◆ **I am seated in the heavenly places with Christ.**

And God raised us up with Christ and seated us with him in the heavenly realms in Christ Jesus. (Ephesians 2:6)

◆ **I am God's workmanship created to produce good works.**

For we are God's workmanship, created in Christ Jesus to do good works, which God prepared in advance for us to do. (Ephesians 2:10)

- I have been brought near to God by the blood of Christ.

  But now in Christ Jesus you who once were far away have been brought near through the blood of Christ. (Ephesians 2:13)

- I am a member of Christ's body and a partaker of his promise.

  This mystery is that through the gospel the Gentiles are heirs together with Israel, members together of one body, and sharers together in the promise in Christ Jesus...for we are members of his body. (Ephesians 3:6; 5:30)

- I have boldness and confident access to God through faith in Christ.

  In him and through faith in him we may approach God with freedom and confidence. (Ephesians 3:12)

- My new self is righteous and holy.

  Put on the new self, created to be like God in true righteousness and holiness. (Ephesians 4:24)

- I was formerly darkness, but now I am light in the Lord.

  For you were once darkness, but now you are light in the Lord. Live as children of light. (Ephesians 5:8)

- I am a citizen of heaven.

  But our citizenship is in heaven. And we eagerly await a Savior from there, the Lord Jesus Christ. (Philippians 3:20)

- The peace of God guards my heart and mind.

  And the peace of God, which transcends all understanding, will guard your hearts and your minds in Christ Jesus. (Philippians 4:7)

- God supplies all my needs.

  And my God will meet all your needs according to his glorious riches in Christ Jesus. (Philippians 4:19)

- **I have been made complete in Christ.**

  You have been given fullness in Christ, who is the head over every power and authority. (Colossians 2:10)

- **I have been raised with Christ.**

  Since, then, you have been raised with Christ, set your hearts on things above, where Christ is seated at the right hand of God. (Colossians 3:1)

- **My life is hidden with Christ in God.**

  For you died, and your life is now hidden with Christ in God. (Colossians 3:3)

- **Christ is my life, and I will be revealed with him in glory.**

  When Christ, who is your life, appears, then you also will appear with him in glory. (Colossians 3:4)

- **I have been chosen of God, and I am holy and beloved.**

  Therefore, as God's chosen people, holy and dearly loved, clothe yourselves with compassion, kindness, humility, gentleness and patience. (Colossians 3:12)

- **God loves me and has chosen me.**

  For we know, brothers loved by God, that he has chosen you. (1 Thessalonians 1:4)

Scripture Memory Summary

Attributes Overview—Matthew 4:19

"Come, follow me," Jesus said, "and I will make you fishers of men."

Attribute One • Learn to Be With Jesus—Matthew 11:28–30

[28] "Come to me, all you who are weary and burdened, and I will give you rest. [29] Take my yoke upon you and learn from me, for I am gentle and humble in heart, and you will find rest for your souls. [30] For my yoke is easy and my burden is light."

Attribute Two • Learn to Listen—Matthew 7:24–25

[24] "Therefore everyone who hears these words of mine and puts them into practice is like a wise man who built his house on the rock. [25] The rain came down, the streams rose, and the winds blew and beat against that house; yet it did not fall, because it had its foundation on the rock."

Attribute Three • Learn to Heal—Matthew 7:7–8

[7] "Ask and it will be given to you; seek and you will find; knock and the door will be opened to you. [8] For everyone who asks receives; he who seeks finds; and to him who knocks, the door will be opened."

Attribute Four • Learn to Influence—Matthew 28:18–20

[18] Then Jesus came to them and said, "All authority in heaven and on earth has been given to me. [19] Therefore go and make disciples of all nations, baptizing them in the name of the Father and of the Son and of the Holy Spirit, [20] and teaching them to obey everything I have commanded you. And surely I am with you always, to the very end of the age."

Attribute Five • Learn to Love—Matthew 22:37–39

[37] Jesus replied: "'Love the Lord your God with all your heart and with all your soul and with all your mind.' [38] This is the first and greatest commandment. [39] And the second is like it: 'Love your neighbor as yourself.'"

Attribute Six • Learn to Pray—Matthew 6:9–13

[9] "This, then, is how you should pray: 'Our Father in heaven, hallowed be your name, [10] your kingdom come, your will be done on earth as it is in heaven. [11] Give us today our daily bread. [12] Forgive us our debts, as we also have forgiven our debtors. [13] And lead us not into temptation, but deliver us from the evil one.'"

Attribute Seven • Learn to Manage—Matthew 6:33

 33 "But seek first his kingdom and his righteousness, and all these things will be given to you as well."

Challenge Memory Verses

Attribute Overview

Proverbs 3:5–6
5 Trust in the LORD with all your heart and lean not on your own understanding; 6 in all your ways acknowledge him, and he will make your paths straight.

Jeremiah 29:11
11 "For I know the plans I have for you," declares the LORD, "plans to prosper you and not to harm you, plans to give you hope and a future."

Attribute One • Learn to Be With Jesus

John 15:5
5 "I am the vine; you are the branches. If a man remains in me and I in him, he will bear much fruit; apart from me you can do nothing."

Matthew 16:24-25
24 Then Jesus said to his disciples, "If anyone would come after me, he must deny himself and take up his cross and follow me. 25 For whoever wants to save his life will lose it, but whoever loses his life for me will find it."

Galatians 2:20
20 I have been crucified with Christ and I no longer live, but Christ lives in me. The life I live in the body, I live by faith in the Son of God, who loved me and gave himself for me.

1 John 1:8-10
8 If we claim to be without sin, we deceive ourselves and the truth is not in us. 9 If we confess our sins, he is faithful and just and will forgive us our sins and purify us from all unrighteousness. 10 If we claim we have not sinned, we make him out to be a liar and his word has no place in our lives.

Learning to Follow Jesus

Attribute Two • Learn to Listen

John 10:27
²⁷ My sheep listen to my voice; I know them, and they follow me.

2 Timothy 3:16-17
¹⁶ All Scripture is God-breathed and is useful for teaching, rebuking, correcting and training in righteousness, ¹⁷ so that the man of God may be thoroughly equipped for every good work.

Psalm 119:11
¹¹ I have hidden your word in my heart that I might not sin against you.

Psalm 119:105
¹⁰⁵ Your word is a lamp to my feet and a light for my path.

1 Corinthians 10:13
¹³ No temptation has seized you except what is common to man. And God is faithful; he will not let you be tempted beyond what you can bear. But when you are tempted, he will also provide a way out so that you can stand up under it.

Luke 6:46
⁴⁶ "Why do you call me, 'Lord, Lord,' and do not do what I say?"

Attribute Three • Learn to Heal

Jeremiah 32:27
²⁷ "I am the LORD, the God of all mankind. Is anything too hard for me?"

2 Corinthians 1:3-4
³ Praise be to the God and Father of our Lord Jesus Christ, the Father of compassion and the God of all comfort, ⁴ who comforts us in all our troubles, so that we can comfort those in any trouble with the comfort we ourselves have received from God.

Psalm 103:2-5
² Praise the LORD, O my soul, and forget not all his benefits— ³ who forgives all your sins and heals all your diseases, ⁴ who redeems your life from the pit and crowns you with love and compassion, ⁵ who satisfies your desires with good things so that your youth is renewed like the eagle's.

1 Peter 2:24

[24] He himself bore our sins in his body on the tree, so that we might die to sins and live for righteousness; by his wounds you have been healed.

Attribute Four • Learn to Influence

Acts 1:8

[8] "But you will receive power when the Holy Spirit comes on you; and you will be my witnesses in Jerusalem, and in all Judea and Samaria, and to the ends of the earth."

John 3:16-17

[16] "For God so loved the world that he gave his one and only Son, that whoever believes in him shall not perish but have eternal life. [17] For God did not send his Son into the world to condemn the world, but to save the world through him."

Ephesians 2:8-10

[8] For it is by grace you have been saved, through faith—and this not from yourselves, it is the gift of God— [9] not by works, so that no one can boast. [10] For we are God's workmanship, created in Christ Jesus to do good works, which God prepared in advance for us to do.

Luke 19:10

[10] "For the Son of Man came to seek and to save what was lost."

2 Peter 3:9

[9] The Lord is not slow in keeping his promise, as some understand slowness. He is patient with you, not wanting anyone to perish, but everyone to come to repentance.

Mark 10:45

[45] For even the Son of Man did not come to be served, but to serve, and to give his life as a ransom for many."

1 John 5:11–12

[11] And this is the testimony: God has given us eternal life, and this life is in his Son. [12] He who has the Son has life; he who does not have the Son of God does not have life.

Romans 10:14–15

[14] How, then, can they call on the one they have not believed in? And how can they believe in the one of whom they have not heard? And how can they hear without someone preaching to them? [15] And how can

they preach unless they are sent? As it is written, "How beautiful are the feet of those who bring good news!"

Attribute Five • Learn to Love

2 Corinthians 5:17
[17] Therefore, if anyone is in Christ, he is a new creation; the old has gone, the new has come!

Psalm 37:4–6
[4] Delight yourself in the LORD and he will give you the desires of your heart. [5] Commit your way to the LORD; trust in him and he will do this: [6] He will make your righteousness shine like the dawn, the justice of your cause like the noonday sun.

Philippians 4:4–7
[4] Rejoice in the Lord always. I will say it again: Rejoice! [5] Let your gentleness be evident to all. The Lord is near. [6] Do not be anxious about anything, but in everything, by prayer and petition, with thanksgiving, present your requests to God. [7] And the peace of God, which transcends all understanding, will guard your hearts and your minds in Christ Jesus.

Lamentations 3:22–25
[22] Because of the LORD's great love we are not consumed, for his compassions never fail. [23] They are new every morning; great is your faithfulness. [24] I say to myself, "The LORD is my portion; therefore I will wait for him." [25] The LORD is good to those whose hope is in him, to the one who seeks him.

Attribute Six • Learn to Pray

Ephesians 6:18
[18] And pray in the Spirit on all occasions with all kinds of prayers and requests. With this in mind, be alert and always keep on praying for all the saints.

1 Timothy 2:1–2
[1] I urge, then, first of all, that requests, prayers, intercession and thanksgiving be made for everyone— [2] for kings and all those in authority, that we may live peaceful and quiet lives in all godliness and holiness.

Jeremiah 33:3
[3] 'Call to me and I will answer you and tell you great and unsearchable things you do not know.'

Isaiah 55:8–11

8 "For my thoughts are not your thoughts, neither are your ways my ways," declares the LORD. 9 "As the heavens are higher than the earth, so are my ways higher than your ways and my thoughts than your thoughts. 10 As the rain and the snow come down from heaven, and do not return to it without watering the earth and making it bud and flourish, so that it yields seed for the sower and bread for the eater, 11 so is my word that goes out from my mouth: It will not return to me empty, but will accomplish what I desire and achieve the purpose for which I sent it."

John 15:7–8

7 If you remain in me and my words remain in you, ask whatever you wish, and it will be given you. 8 This is to my Father's glory, that you bear much fruit, showing yourselves to be my disciples.

Attribute Seven • Learn to Manage

Matthew 6:19–21

19 "Do not store up for yourselves treasures on earth, where moth and rust destroy, and where thieves break in and steal. 20 But store up for yourselves treasures in heaven, where moth and rust do not destroy, and where thieves do not break in and steal. 21 For where your treasure is, there your heart will be also."

Proverbs 16:3

3 Commit to the LORD whatever you do, and your plans will succeed.

Proverbs 3:9–10

9 Honor the LORD with your wealth, with the firstfruits of all your crops; 10 then your barns will be filled to overflowing, and your vats will brim over with new wine.

Titus 1:7–9

7 Since an overseer is entrusted with God's work, he must be blameless—not overbearing, not quick-tempered, not given to drunkenness, not violent, not pursuing dishonest gain. 8 Rather he must be hospitable, one who loves what is good, who is self-controlled, upright, holy and disciplined. 9 He must hold firmly to the trustworthy message as it has been taught, so that he can encourage others by sound doctrine and refute those who oppose it.

Selected Bibliography

* Indicates the recommended first book to read on an attribute.

Attribute One • Learn to Be With Jesus

Barton, Ruth Haley. *Sacred Rhythms: Arranging Our Lives for Spiritual Transformation.* InterVarsity, 2006.

Blackaby, Henry, Richard Blackaby, and Claude King. *Experiencing God,* rev. ed. Nashville: Broadman & Holman, 2008.

Bonhoeffer, Dietrich. *Life Together.* New York: Harper and Row, 1976.

————. *The Cost of Discipleship.* Riverside, NJ: MacMillan Publishing, 1967.

Brother Lawrence, *The Practice of the Presence of God.* New York: Doubleday, 1977.

*Foster, Richard. *Celebration of Discipline.* San Francisco: Harper, 1988.

Law, William. *A Serious Call to a Devout and Holy Life.* Philadelphia: Westminster, 1955.

Merton, Thomas. *Contemplative Prayer.* Garden City, NY: Doubleday and Co., 1971.

Murray, Andrew. *Abide in Christ.* New York: Whitaker House, 2002.

Sheldon, Charles. *In His Steps.* Nashville, TN: Broadman, 1935.

Smith, Gordon T. *The Voice of Jesus: Discernment, Prayer, and the Witness of the Spirit.* Downers Grove, IL: InterVarsity, 2003.

Willard, Dallas. *Spirit of the Disciplines.* San Francisco: Harper and Row, 1991 (1990).

Attribute Two • Learn to Listen

Chamber, Oswald. *My Utmost for His Highest.* New York: Mead, 1935.

*Fee, Gordon and Douglas Stuart. *How to Read the Bible for All Its Worth.* Grand Rapids: Zondervan, 2003.

Hendricks, Howard G. and William D. Hendricks, *Living By the Book.* Chicago: Moody, 1991.

Attribute Three • Learn to Heal

Anderson, Neil. *The Bondage Breaker.* Eugene, OR: Harvest House Publishers, 1993.

Baker, John. *Life's Healing Choices: Freedom from Your Hurts, Hang-ups, and Habits.* New York: Howard Books, 2007.

Bosworth, F. F. *Christ the Healer.* Old Tappan, NJ: Fleming, 1973.

Cloud, Henry and John Townsend. *Boundaries.* Grand Rapids: Zondervan, 1992.

*Richards, James. *How to Stop the Pain.* New Kensington, PA: Whitaker House, 2001.

Sande, Ken. *The Peace Maker.* Grand Rapids: Baker, 2004.

Seamands, David A. *Healing for Damaged Emotions.* Colorado Springs: David C. Cook, 1981.

Attribute Four • Learn to Influence

Aldrich, Joe. *Life-Style Evangelism.* Sisters, OR: Multnomah, 2006.

Carnegie, Dale. *How to Win Friends & Influence People.* New York: Pocket Books, 1936.

Cox, Harvey. *Fire from Heaven.* New York: Addison-Wesley, 1995.

Deere, Jack. *Surprised By the Power of the Spirit.* Grand Rapids: Zondervan, 1993.

Egli, Jim and Ben Hoerr. *The I-Factor.* Houston: Touch Publications, 1993.

Fee, Gordon. *God's Empowering Presence.* Peabody, MA: Hendrickson, 1994.

Ford, Leighton. *Good News Is for Sharing.* Elgin, IL: David C. Cook, 1977.

Greenfield, John. *Power from on High.* Muskegon, MI: Dust to Ashes Publications, 1996.

Gumbel, Nicky. *Questions of Life.* Colorado Springs: David C. Cook, 2004.

Hurst, Randy. *The Helper.* Springfield, MO: Gospel Publishing House, 2004.

*Hybels, Bill and Mark Middelberg. *Becoming a Contagious Christian.* Grand Rapids: Eerdmans, 1994.

Kinnaman, David and Gabe Lyons. *UnChristian.* Grand Rapids: Baker, 2007.

Lewis, C. S. *Mere Christianity.* New York: Macmillan, 1960.

Little, Paul. *Know Why You Believe.* Wheaton: Victor Books, 1974.

———. *How to Give Away Your Faith.* Downers Grove, IL: InterVarsity Press, 1988.

McDowell, Josh. *More Than a Carpenter.* Wheaton: Tyndale, 1977.

McLaren, Brian. *Finding Faith.* Grand Rapids: Zondervan, 2007.

———. *More Ready Than You Realize.* Grand Rapids: Zondervan, 2002.

Menzies, William W. and Robert P. Menzies. *Spirit and Power.* Grand Rapids: Zondervan, 2000.

Nouwen, Henri. *In the Name of Jesus.* New York: Crossroads Publishing Company, 1992.

Pippert, Rebecca Manley. *Out of the Salt Shaker and Into the World.* Downers Grove, IL: InterVarsity Press, 1979.

Sherrill, John L. *They Speak with Other Tongues.* New York: Jove, 1964.

Strobel, Lee. *A Case for a Creator.* Grand Rapids: Zondervan, 2004.

———. *A Case For Christ.* Grand Rapids: Zondervan, 1998.

———. *A Case For Faith.* Grand Rapids: Zondervan, 2000.

Wood, George O. *Living in the Spirit.* Springfield, MO: 2009.

Attribute Five • Learn to Love

Crabb, Larry. *Finding God.* Grand Rapids: Zondervan, 1993.

*McGee, Robert. *The Search for Significance.* Houston: Rapha Publishing, 1990.

Mahaney, C. J. *The Cross Centered Life.* Sisters, OR: Multnomah, 2002.

Packer, J. I. *Knowing God.* Downers Grove, IL: InterVarsity Press, 1973.

Learning to Follow Jesus

Attribute Six • Learn to Pray

Bounds, E.M. *A Treasury of Prayer.* Minneapolis: Bethany Fellowship, Inc., 1960.

Eastman, Dick. *The Hour That Changes the World.* Grand Rapids: Baker, 1978.

Foster, Richard J. *Prayer.* San Francisco: Harper, 1992.

Grubb, Norman P. *Rees Howells Intercessor.* Philadelphia: Christian Literature Crusade, 1952.

* Hybels, Bill. *Too Busy Not To Pray.* Downers Grove: InterVarsity Press, 1988.

Murray, Andrew. *With Christ in the School of Prayer.* Philadelphia: H. Altemus, 1895.

Yancey, Philip. *Prayer: Does It Make Any Difference?* Grand Rapids: Zondervan, 2006.

Attribute Seven • Learn to Manage

Carnegie, Dale. *How to Win Friends & Influence People.* New York: Pocket Books, 1936.

Covey, Stephen. *The 7 Habits of Highly Effective People.* New York: Simon & Schuster, 1989.

Duncan, Todd. *Time Traps.* Nashville: Thomas Nelson, 2004.

* MacDonald, Gordon. *Ordering Your Private World.* Nashville: Thomas Nelson, 1984.

Maxwell, John C. *Developing the Leader Within You.* Nashville: Thomas Nelson, 1993.

———. *The Winning Attitude.* Nashville: Thomas Nelson, 1993.

Ramsey, Dave. *Total Money Makeover.* Nashville: Thomas Nelson, 2007.

Smith, Hyrum W. *The 10 Natural Laws of Successful Time and Life Management.* New York: Warner Brothers, 1994.

Swenson, Richard A. *Margin: Restoring Emotional, Physical, Financial, and Time Reserves to Overloaded Lives.* Colorado Springs: NavPress, 1992.

———. *The Overload Syndrome: Learning to Live Within Your Limits.* Colorado Springs: NavPress, 1998.

Winston, Stephanie. *Getting Organized.* New York: Grand Central Publishing, 2006.

www.mypyramid.gov

Spiritual Coaching Resources

What is a Spiritual Coach?

A spiritual coach is one who comes alongside another person to help him or her become an authentic follower of Christ.

- **Coming Alongside**
  - You are on the journey with the person. You are not over the person.
  - Assume an attitude of humility. We are all learning to follow Jesus.
- **Helping**
  - You are there to help.
  - You won't have all the answers.
  - The focus is on the person being coached and not the coach.
- **Authentic Follower of Christ**
  - The goal is that the other person will be an authentic follower of Jesus.
  - The goal is not the completion of material. It is growing in the seven attributes of the follower of Jesus.

What is the Role of a Spiritual Coach?

- To help the person continue to move along the path to following Christ

  Hebrews 10:24, [24]"And let us consider how we may spur one another on toward love and good deeds."

- To gently challenge a person to become an authentic follower of Jesus

  Proverbs 27:17, [17]"As iron sharpens iron, so one man sharpens another."

What is the Process of Spiritual Coaching?[1]

* **Relate**—establish coaching relationship and agenda
* **Reflect**—discover and explore key issues
* **Refocus**—determine priorities and action steps
* **Resource**—provide support and encouragement
* **Review**—evaluate, celebrate, and revise plans

What Types of Questions Will I Ask as a Spiritual Coach?

* **Relate**
    * How are you doing?
    * How was your week?
* **Reflect**
    * What stood out to you this week in your reading?
    * What obstacles are you facing?
* **Refocus**
    * What would you like to do?
    * What are some possible ways to get there?
* **Resource**
    * What resources do you have?
    * What resources are you missing?
    * Would you like some accountability around that?
* **Review**
    * What's working?
    * What's not working?
    * What needs to change?

Getting Started
Coaching Session

1. Introduce yourself if you don't know the person.

2. Turn to the "Getting Started" page and emphasize the following:

   a. Congratulate them—choosing to follow Jesus is the most important decision of their life.

   b. Explain the importance of coming to Christ, hearing his words, and putting them into practice (doing).

   c. Explain the importance of getting involved in a small group.

   d. Explain that you are their spiritual coach. Let them know if, for any reason, they would rather have a different coach, that will be fine with you. You will not be offended. Getting a coach with whom you have good chemistry is important.

   e. Talk about the importance of setting aside about fifteen minutes a day for time with God. Ask them when that will work best. (See the fill in for this.) Have them write it in the book.

   f. Encourage them to write in their book. It will help them apply more to their life.

   g. Make sure the person has a Bible in a modern translation (NIV, TNIV, NLT).

   h. Show them how to do the Scripture memory—drop a word.

      1. Encourage them to pray before they start.
      2. Remind them that the key is reviewing daily.
      3. Tell them you will quiz them when you get together.

3. Review the Seven Attributes from the Table of Contents.

    a. Encourage them to read one a day.

    b. Show them how each of the seven attributes has a chapter and steps all its own.

4. Ask him or her if they have any questions.

5. Ask how you can pray for them.

    a. You may want to write this down and pray for them during the week.

    b. Take the person by the hand (for men the hand shake posture is non-threatening).

    c. Pray that God will bless this person as he or she takes the next steps as a follower of Christ.

6. Exchange phone numbers and e-mail addresses.

7. Set a time for the next meeting(s).

    a. It is best to get a weekly time of about an hour that works for both of you.

    b. Try to schedule out for one or two months if possible.

Attribute Overview
Coaching Session

Coaches' Note: The Attribute Overview Coaching Session will probably take two to three sessions. Let the person set the pace.

Relate

- How was your week?
  - Share briefly about your week if it seems appropriate.
  - Express what an honor it is to be able to walk alongside them on their journey as a follower of Christ.
  - Explain your role as a spiritual coach—to come alongside and help him or her become an authentic follower of Christ.
- Get to know the person
  - Where were you born and raised?
  - Tell me a little bit about your family (parents, spouse, children).
  - What is your work?
- Share your faith journey.
  - As we start on this journey together, it might be helpful for you to know a little bit about my faith journey.
  - *Important:* It is very important that they hear how Jesus changed your life. This should be a 5–10 minute testimony maximum.
- Tell me about your faith journey.
- How did you decide to make a commitment to Christ?
  - Be a good listener.
  - Express appropriate emotion but don't side track the conversation. *page 254*

⟩ Summarize what you hear them saying.

⟩ Be sensitive to the leading the Holy Spirit.

⟩ Don't push if they decide to say things vaguely.

Reflect

• How did it go this week in your reading?

• Were you able to find a small group that worked for you?

• How did it go with your 5–15 minutes each day with the Lord?

• Were you able to memorize Matthew 4:19?

⟩ "Come, follow me," Jesus said, "and I will make you fishers of men." Matthew 4:19

• Which of the attributes stood out to you the most?

Refocus

Attribute Two • Learn to Listen talked about repentance.

• Was that an encouraging section for you?

• Do you feel comfortable sharing with me some things from which you are repenting?

• What would you like to do about those things?

Resource

• Would you like me to ask you about this next week?

Attribute Three • Learn to Heal

• Is there anything about which I can pray for healing for you?

Attribute Six • Learn to Pray

• Do you think the Lord spoke to you in some way this week?

Refocus

Attribute Seven • Learn to Manage

- What are some places or areas of your life in which you need to invest so that your heart goes where you want it to go?
- What are you going to invest in for each of these areas?

Resource

- Would you like me to ask you about this next week?

Prayer

- How can I pray for you today?
  - Write down their prayer requests on a Prayer Request List in the back of this book. Be sure to write the date it was answered as well.
  - Take them by the hand (for men the hand shake posture is not threatening).
  - Pray for what they asked and that God would bless them as they take the next steps as a follower of Christ.

Review

- Is this helping you in your walk with Jesus?

Set the date and time for the next meeting

- Does this time work for you?
  - Set a day and time for the next meeting(s).
  - Schedule out for 1–2 months if possible.

Attribute One • Learn to Be With Jesus
Coaching Session

Relate

+ How are things going?

Review

+ Were you able to find a small group that worked for you?

+ How did it go with your 5–15 minutes each day with the Lord?

+ Do you still remember Matthew 4:19?
    ⇢ "Come, follow me," Jesus said, "and I will make you fishers of men." Matthew 4:19

+ Can you recite Matthew 11:28–30?
    ⇢ [28] "Come to me, all you who are weary and burdened, and I will give you rest. [29] Take my yoke upon you and learn from me, for I am gentle and humble in heart, and you will find rest for your souls. [30] For my yoke is easy and my burden is light." Matthew 11:28–30

Reflect

+ What stood out to you this week in your reading?

+ Step 1—Were you able to download any songs from iTunes? Do you need help doing that?

+ How is your Bible reading going?

+ What kinds of things stood out to you as you read?

Refocus

+ Did you make any decisions to do something as a result of what stood out to you?

Resource

- Do you need any support to help you with your decisions?

Coaches' Note: See the "How to Develop a Schedule" resource in the Resource section if the person needs help with his or her schedule.

Review

- Did anything confuse you this week as you read?

Prayer

- How can I pray for you this week?
    - Turn to the prayer list you started for this person.
    - Ask if God has answered their requests from the previous week.
    - Take them by the hand (for men the hand shake posture is not threatening).
    - Pray for what they asked and that God would bless them as they take the next steps as a follower of Christ.

Set the date and time for the next meeting

- Schedule out for 1–2 months if possible.

Attribute Two • Learn to Listen
Coaching Session

Relate

• What was the highlight of your week?

Review

• How did it go this week with your time with God?

• What challenges did have in spending time with God?

• Were you able to find a small group that worked for you?

• How is it going with Matthew 4:19?
  ⤑ "Come, follow me," Jesus said, "and I will make you fishers of men." Matthew 4:19

• How about Matthew 11:28–30?
  ⤑ [28] "Come to me, all you who are weary and burdened, and I will give you rest. [29] Take my yoke upon you and learn from me, for I am gentle and humble in heart, and you will find rest for your souls. [30] For my yoke is easy and my burden is light." Matthew 11:28–30

• How is Matthew 7:24–25 coming?
  ⤑ [24] "Therefore everyone who hears these words of mine and puts them into practice is like a wise man who built his house on the rock. [25] The rain came down, the streams rose, and the winds blew and beat against that house; yet it did not fall, because it had its foundation on the rock." Matthew 7:24–25

Reflect

• What stood out to you this week in your reading?

Refocus

- Have you thought about how you are going to incorporate Bible reading into your life?
- Do you have specific questions about God for which you could use an answer?
  - → **Coaches' Note:** Listen but don't give answers if you don't have them.
- Do you have some things you need to adjust so you can be more productive for God?
- What are some obstacles you face in doing that?

Resource

- What do you need to make that happen?
- Would you like some accountability around that?
- What would accountability look like for you?

Prayer

- How can I pray for you this week?
  - → Turn to the prayer list you started for this person.
  - → Ask if God has answered their requests from the previous week.
  - → Take them by the hand (for men the hand shake posture is not threatening).
  - → Pray for what they asked and that God would bless them as they take the next steps as a follower of Christ.

Set the date and time for the next meeting

- Schedule out for 1–2 months if possible.

Attribute Three • Learn to Heal
Coaching Session

Relate

• How is your week going?

Review

• What's working? Not working? Missing? Confused?

Reflect

• What stood out to you from the reading this week?

Refocus

• In what area(s) of your life would you like healing?
  Coaches' Note: Take time to pray right now for healing.

Resource

• What could you do to promote healing in your life?
  Coaches' Note: The person should know they can do
  the following:
  ⇢ Ask God to heal them
  ⇢ See a doctor if it is something medical
  ⇢ Learn about a helpful healing process (Grief,
    Conflict Resolution, Recovery)
• What resources do you need to find healing?

Prayer

• How can I pray for you this week?
  ⇢ Turn to the prayer list you started for this person.
  ⇢ Ask if God has answered their requests from the
    previous week.

• Does anyone around you need healing?
  ⇢ Take them by the hand (for men the hand shake
    posture is not threatening).
  ⇢ Pray for what they asked and that God would

bless them as they take the next steps as a follower of Christ.

Set the date and time for the next meeting

• Schedule out for 1–2 months if possible.

Attribute Four • Learn to Influence
Coaching Session

Relate
+ What's going on in your life this week?

Review
+ How is your follow process going?

Reflect
+ Did you have a chance to fill out the Evangelism Styles Questionnaire? What was your style?
+ Did you make out your prayer list? Did you begin to pray? Did anything happen?
+ Did you enjoy writing out your story?
+ What did you think about the discussion about the Baptism in the Holy Spirit? Is that something you have experienced? Would like to experience? If yes, encourage them to draw near to Jesus, to wait for the Holy Spirit to come upon them, and to yield to the Spirit's promptings.

Refocus
+ In what ways would you like to grow as a result of what you learned this week?

Resource
+ What do you need to make that happen?
+ How can I support you in that?

Prayer
+ How can I pray for you this week?
  ⁕ Turn to the prayer list you started for this person.
  ⁕ Ask if they would like you to pray for them to receive the Baptism in the Holy Spirit.
  ⁕ Pray for what they asked and that God would bless them as they take the next steps as a follower of Christ.

Set the date and time for the next meeting.

Attribute Five • Learn to Love
Coaching Session

Relate

• What's new in your life this week?

Review

• Were you able to pray for people on your influence list this week?

• Did anything unusual happen with any of those relationships?

Reflect

• Did you take the assessments this week before you worked on each step?

• Were you low on any of the assessments? Did you agree with the summary?

Refocus

• What would you like to do as a result of what you learned in Attribute Five?

• What are some possible ways of doing that?

Resource

• What resources do you have to make that change?

• Do you see any obstacles to making that change?

• Would you like some accountability around that?

• What would that look like for you?

Prayer

• How can I pray for you this week?
  ◦ Turn to the prayer list you started for this person.
  ◦ Ask if God has answered their requests from the previous week.

✢ Pray for what they asked and that God would bless them as they take the next steps as a follower of Christ.

Set the date and time for the next meeting

Attribute Six • Learn to Pray
Coaching Session

Relate

- What was the highlight of your week?

Review

- How did it go with your thought process this week? (loving God, identifying any lies, replacing the lies with the truth)

- Do you feel like you made some progress?

Reflect

- What stood out to you as you worked through this attribute?

- On Step 2, there was a discussion about areas that we have difficulty giving up control. Did you have any areas you would like to discuss?

- On Step 3, there was a discussion about food. How are you with food?

- What did you think about the process for "Praying Through Pain" on Step 4? Do you have any areas you prayed through or would like to pray through that you want to talk about?

- Did you have any trouble identifying the lie?

- On Step 5, there was a discussion about "praying in the Spirit" Do you have any experience with praying in a prayer language? Is that something you would like to talk about?

Refocus

- What would you like to do as a result of what you read and learned this week?

Resource

• What resources do you need to make that happen?

Prayer

• How can I pray for you this week?
  ⇢ Turn to the prayer list you started for this person.
  ⇢ Ask if God has answered their requests from the previous week.
  ⇢ Pray for what they asked and that God would bless them as they take the next steps as a follower of Christ.

Set the date and time for the next meeting

Attribute Seven • Learn to Manage
Coaching Session

Relate

- How are you doing?

Review

- How is your prayer life coming?
- Have you been able to keep your quiet time consistent this week?
- Did you learn anything in your prayer life this week?

Reflect

- How did it go with the Learn to Manage attribute?
- Are there any key areas that stood out to you?

Refocus

- Did you identify any steps you would like to take with putting God first in your finances?
- How about with your body?
- How is your time management?

Resource

- Is that something with which you would like some support?
- What do you need to get where you want to go in these areas?

Prayer

- How can I pray for you this week?
  - Turn to the prayer list you started for this person.
  - Ask if God has answered their requests from the previous week.
  - Pray for what they asked and that God would bless them as they take the next steps as a follower of Christ.

Set the date and time for the next meeting

Coaching Certification
Questions

Learn to Be With Jesus
+ Are you faithful in attendance at the Sunday morning service?
+ Are you involved in a small group?
+ Do you spend at least 15 minutes alone with Jesus?

Learn to Listen
+ Do you read God's word daily?
+ Do you regularly apply God's word to your daily life?

Learn to Heal
+ Do you regularly pray for healing?
+ Is your faith growing about healing?

Learn to Influence
+ Do you have a list of family, friends, coworkers, and neighbors for whom you pray at least weekly?
+ Do you know your primary mode of evangelism?
+ How are you utilizing your primary mode of evangelism?
+ Are you serving your family faithfully?
+ Is Jesus honored by how you work on the job?
+ Would people consider you a model employee?
+ Would you tell me your 3 minute testimony?
+ Have you videotaped your testimony?
+ Do you listen to people more than you talk?

Learn to Love
+ Do you feel loved and accepted by God?
+ Do you accept people?
+ Do you know how to live free from anxiety?

Learn to Pray
- Do you pray daily?
- Do you have a prayer list?
- Do you walk in forgiveness?
- Do you enjoy worshiping God?

Learn to Manage
- Do you get enough sleep?
- Do you attempt to eat healthy?
- Do you exercise?
- Are you free from life controlling habits?
- Do you use your spiritual gifts?
- Are you careful with your words?
- Do you keep your word?
- Do you manage your time well?
- Are you living within your financial means?
- Do you seek God first in your finances?
- Are you managing your finances in a way that honors God?

Notes

Attribute Three • Overview

1. There was nothing that Jesus could not heal. Jesus healed diseases and sicknesses. He also set people free who were dominated by forces of evil.

Attribute Four • Overview

1. Rick Warren, *The Purpose-Driven® Life* (Grand Rapids: Zondervan, 2002), 17.

Attribute Five • Overview

1. See Attribute Six–Step 4, "Learn to Pray Through Pain."

Attribute One • Step Three

1. Some find once they become followers of Jesus, they are very hungry to read God's Word. If you are up for the challenge, you can read through the entire Bible in one year by reading about twenty minutes per day. Check out www.unboundbible.blogspot.com for a yearly Bible reading plan that some of the Spring Valley Community Church family use.

Attribute Two • Step One

1. Haddon Robinson, *What Jesus Said About Successful Living* (Grand Rapids: Discovery House Publishers, 1991), 28.

2. Ibid.

Attribute Two • Step Four

1. If you found Deuteronomy 6:16, you are correct.

Attribute Three • Step One

1. http://www.time.com/time/magazine/article/0,9171,982784-1,00.html.

Attribute Three • Step Five

1. I recommend *When God Doesn't Make Sense* (Wheaton: Tyndale House Publishers, 1997) by James Dobson and *Where Is God When It Hurts* (Grand Rapids: Zondervan, 1990) by Philip Yancey.

Attribute Four • Introduction

1. Unfortunately different groups have polarized about speaking in tongues. Some make "speaking in tongues" the point of the baptism in the Holy Spirit. A simple reading of Acts 1:8 indicates otherwise. Speaking in tongues was the normal part of that experience but not the emphasis. The repetition of the experience throughout the New Testament (Acts 10, 19; 1 Corinthians 12–14)

indicates it was a normal part of the early church and was the expected and normal experience. The purpose of the empowerment of the Spirit is to enable people to effectively witness for Christ. Others argue the experience is not valid for the Christian today, is not expected, and should be avoided. A plain reading of Scripture indicates that empowerment for witnessing was the focus of the experience. The polarization in the church about the issue of speaking in tongues does not honor Jesus. Speaking in tongues is neither a spiritual badge to be worn with pride nor an experience that should be avoided. It is a blessing and a by-product of the empowerment of the Holy Spirit.

Attribute Four • Step One

1. Win and Charles Arn surveyed 14,000 people nationwide to ask them, "What or who was responsible for your coming to Christ?" At least 75 percent of respondents in every context said a friend or a family member was the most significant influence.

2. http://www.barna.org/barna-update/article/5-barna-update/196-evangelism-is-most-effective-among-kids.

3. 80 percent of the people surveyed by Thom Rainer indicated that they would attend a church if they were asked (*The UnChurched Next Door*, Grand Rapids: Zondervan, 2008), 32.

Attribute Five • Introduction

1. Robert McGee, *The Search for Significance* (Houston: Rapha Publishing, 1985), 100.

Attribute Five • Step Three

1. Robert S. McGee, *The Search for Significance*, 84

2. Ibid., 85.

Attribute Five • Step Four

1. Robert McGee, *The Search for Significance*, 108-110.

Attribute Six • Step Two

1. Peter Furler and Steve Taylor. "He Reigns" (Ariose Music. Admin. by EMI CMG Publishing, 2003).

2. David Crowder. "O Praise Him" (worshiptogether.com Songs. Sixsteps Music. both admin. by EMI CMG Publishing, 2003).

3. Marc Byrd and Steve Hindalong. "God of Wonders" (New Spring Publishing, Inc. Never Say Never Songs. both admin. by Brentwood-Benson Music Publishing, Inc. Storm Boy Music. Meaux Mercy. both admin. by EMI CMG Publishing, 2000).

4. Laura Story and Jesse Reeves. "Indescribable" (Worshiptogether.com Songs. Sixsteps Music. Gleaning Publishing. admin. by EMI CMG Publishing, 2004).

Attribute Six • Step Four

1. There are more than sixty lament psalms. There are individual laments (e.g. 3, 22, 31, 42, 57, 69, 71, 120, 139, and 142) and corporate laments (e.g. 12, 44, 80, 94, and 137). The lament usually exhibits the following pattern: Address the LORD; Complain; statement of Trust in the LORD; expectation of Deliverance; Assurance of the LORD's victory; and Praise for the LORD (Gordon Fee and Douglas Stewart, *How to Read the Bible for All Its Worth* [Grand Rapids: Zondervan, 2003]).

Attribute Six • Step Five

1. Martha Raddatz, *The Long Road Home* (New York: G. P. Putnam's Sons, 2007).

Attribute Seven • Step One

1. Walter F. Arndt and F. Wilbur Gingrich, *A Greek-English Lexicon of the New Testament* (Chicago: The University of Chicago Press, 1979), 475.

2. I am not sure to whom this quote belongs. It has been attributed to Ralph Waldo Emerson (1803–1882), Charles Reade (1814–1884), and a Buddist Proverb.

Attribute Seven • Step Two

1. This was discussed in Overview Attribute Seven.

2. Www.crown.org and www.daveramsey.com are good places to start.

Attribute Seven • Step Five

1. I (Daniel) first heard about this story in Richard Swenson's book, *The Overload Syndrome* (Colorado Springs: NavPress, 1998), 23–24.

2. My friend, Bryan Koch, pastor of Glad Tidings in Reading, Pennsylvania, did a couple of excellent teaching series entitled, "Slaying the Monster of More" and "If I Were a Rich Man" that are worth listening to. You can find them in the resource section of www.gtaog.org.

3. Proverbs 6:6–11, 10:26, 13:4, 15:19, 19:24, 20:4, 21:25–26, 22:13, 24:30–34, 26:13–16.

Resources • Attribute Three

1. David H. Olson, *Prepare/Enrich Counselor's Manual* (Minneapolis: Life Innovations, Inc, 1982, 1986, 1996), 63–64.

2. Elisabeth Kubler-Ross and David Kessler, *On Grief and Grieving: Finding the Meaning of Grief Through the Five Stages of Loss* (New York: Scribner, 2005).

3. http://www.celebraterecovery.com.

Resources • Attribute Four

1. Taken from ***Becoming a Contagious Christian Participant's Guide*** by LEE P. STROBEL; BILL HYBELS; MARK MITTELBERG. Copyright © 1995, 2007

by Willow Creek Community Church. Used by permission of Zondervan. WWW.ZONDERVAN.COM.

Resources • Attribute Five

1. Robert S. McGee, *The Search for Significance* (Houston: Rapha Publishing, 1985), 46–47. Used by permission.

2. Ibid., 66–67.

3. Ibid., 90–91.

4. Ibid., 105–106.

5. Ibid., 40–41.

Spiritual Coaching Resources

1. The coaching model adopted in this resource, particularly the 5Rs of coaching, comes from *Coaching 101* by Robert E. Logan, Sherilyn Carlton, and Tara Miller (ChurchSmart Resources, 2003). Used by permission.

Scripture Reference Index

Topical Index

Prayer Request List

Request	Date	Date Answered

Prayer Request List

Request   **Date**   **Date Answered**

Prayer Request List

Request	Date	Date Answered
....		
....		
....		
....		
....		
....		
....		
....		
....		
....		
....		
....		
....		
....		
....		
....		
....		
....		
....		
....		
....		
....		
....		
....		
....		
....		
....		
....		
....		
....		
....		